OPPOSING
VIEWPOINTS®
SERIES

W9-ADJ-851

Renewable Energy

Other Books of Related Interest:

Opposing Viewpoints Series
Conserving the Environment

Energy Alternatives

Current Controversies Series
Alternative Energy Sources

Conserving the Environment

Pollution

"Congress shall make no law. . .abridging the freedom of speech, or of the press."

First Amendment to the U.S. Constitution

The basic foundation of our democracy is the First Amendment guarantee of freedom of expression. The *Opposing Viewpoints* Series is dedicated to the concept of this basic freedom and the idea that it is more important to practice it than to enshrine it.

Renewable Energy

Jacqueline Langwith, Book Editor

GREENHAVEN PRESS
A part of Gale, Cengage Learning

Detroit • New York • San Francisco • New Haven, Conn • Waterville, Maine • London

Christine Nasso, *Publisher*
Elizabeth Des Chenes, *Managing Editor*

© 2009 Greenhaven Press, a part of Gale, Cengage Learning

LIBRARY OF CONGRESS CATALOGING-IN-PUBLICATION DATA

Renewable energy / Jacqueline Langwith, book editor.
  p. cm. -- (Opposing viewpoints)
  Includes bibliographical references and index.
  ISBN 978-0-7377-4226-8 (hardcover)
  ISBN 978-0-7377-4227-5 (pbk.)
  1. Renewable energy sources--Juvenile literature. I. Langwith, Jacqueline.
  TJ808.2.R44 2008
  333.79'4--dc22
                                                    2008020845

Printed in the United States of America
2 3 4 5 6   13 12 11 10 09

ED112

Contents

Chapter 1: What Is Renewable Energy?

Chapter 2: Is Renewable Energy Beneficial?

Chapter 3: What Are the Benefits of Ethanol as a Renewable Transportation Fuel?

Chapter 4: How Should the Government Promote Renewable Energy and Fuels?

Why Consider Opposing Viewpoints?

> *"The only way in which a human being can make some approach to knowing the whole of a subject is by hearing what can be said about it by persons of every variety of opinion and studying all modes in which it can be looked at by every character of mind. No wise man ever acquired his wisdom in any mode but this."*
>
> John Stuart Mill

In our media-intensive culture it is not difficult to find differing opinions. Thousands of newspapers and magazines and dozens of radio and television talk shows resound with differing points of view. The difficulty lies in deciding which opinion to agree with and which "experts" seem the most credible. The more inundated we become with differing opinions and claims, the more essential it is to hone critical reading and thinking skills to evaluate these ideas. *Opposing Viewpoints* books address this problem directly by presenting stimulating debates that can be used to enhance and teach these skills. The varied opinions contained in each book examine many different aspects of a single issue. While examining these conveniently edited opposing views, readers can develop critical thinking skills such as the ability to compare and contrast authors' credibility, facts, argumentation styles, use of persuasive techniques, and other stylistic tools. In short, the *Opposing Viewpoints* series is an ideal way to attain the higher-level thinking and reading skills so essential in a culture of diverse and contradictory opinions.

In addition to providing a tool for critical thinking, *Opposing Viewpoints* books challenge readers to question their own strongly held opinions and assumptions. Most people form their opinions on the basis of upbringing, peer pressure, and personal, cultural, or professional bias. By reading carefully balanced opposing views, readers must directly confront new ideas as well as the opinions of those with whom they disagree. This is not to simplistically argue that everyone who reads opposing views will—or should—change his or her opinion. Instead, the series enhances readers' understanding of their own views by encouraging confrontation with opposing ideas. Careful examination of others' views can lead to the readers' understanding of the logical inconsistencies in their own opinions, perspective on why they hold an opinion, and the consideration of the possibility that their opinion requires further evaluation.

Evaluating Other Opinions

To ensure that this type of examination occurs, *Opposing Viewpoints* books present all types of opinions. Prominent spokespeople on different sides of each issue as well as well-known professionals from many disciplines challenge the reader. An additional goal of the series is to provide a forum for other, less known, or even unpopular viewpoints. The opinion of an ordinary person who has had to make the decision to cut off life support from a terminally ill relative, for example, may be just as valuable and provide just as much insight as a medical ethicist's professional opinion. The editors have two additional purposes in including these less known views. One, the editors encourage readers to respect others' opinions—even when not enhanced by professional credibility. It is only by reading or listening to and objectively evaluating others' ideas that one can determine whether they are worthy of consideration. Two, the inclusion of such viewpoints encourages the important critical thinking skill of objectively evaluating an author's credentials and bias. This evaluation will illuminate an author's reasons for taking a particular stance on an issue and will aid in readers' evaluation of the author's ideas.

It is our hope that these books will give readers a deeper understanding of the issues debated and an appreciation of the complexity of even seemingly simple issues when good and honest people disagree. This awareness is particularly important in a democratic society such as ours in which people enter into public debate to determine the common good. Those with whom one disagrees should not be regarded as enemies but rather as people whose views deserve careful examination and may shed light on one's own.

Thomas Jefferson once said that "difference of opinion leads to inquiry, and inquiry to truth." Jefferson, a broadly educated man, argued that "if a nation expects to be ignorant and free. . .it expects what never was and never will be." As individuals and as a nation, it is imperative that we consider the opinions of others and examine them with skill and discernment. The *Opposing Viewpoints* series is intended to help readers achieve this goal.

David L. Bender and Bruno Leone,
Founders

Introduction

> *"Fossil fuels—coal, oil and natural gas— currently provide more than 85% of all the energy consumed in the United States, nearly two-thirds of our electricity, and virtually all of our transportation fuels. Moreover, it is likely that the nation's reliance on fossil fuels to power an expanding economy will actually increase over at least the next two decades even with aggressive development and deployment of new renewable and nuclear technologies." —U.S. Department of Energy*

> *"It's not going to be easy, but we have to move away from the carbon economy."*
> *—Bill Clinton,*
> *42nd president of the United States,*
> *November 2007*

From the twentieth century onward, the world marketplace has depended on substances formed millions of years ago and buried deep under the earth. A vast number of things encountered in day-to-day life, such as toothpaste, deodorant, computers, TVs, basketballs, tires, and tennis rackets, are made from carbon. Going to the store and buying these things, or ordering them online and having them delivered, require the use of trains, trucks, or planes powered with carbonaceous fuels. Carbonaceous fuels are also used to provide heat and electricity. Coal, oil, and natural gas are the carbonaceous substances that fuel the world's economy.

Coal, oil, and natural gas are called fossil fuels because they were formed from the remains of plants and animals that lived hundreds of millions of years ago, before the age of dinosaurs. When these ancient life forms died, they accumulated and were buried by deeper and deeper layers of sediment. The actual transformation process of these prehistoric creatures into coal, oil, and natural gas is not known. But scientists do know that pressure (from being buried deep underground), heat, and a great deal of time went into the making of fossil fuels. Scientists believe that oil and natural gas come from the remains of ancient ocean-dwelling creatures, while coal was formed primarily from the remains of trees and terrestrial animals. Fossil fuels have been found virtually everywhere on the planet except Antarctica.

Ancient humans were aware of, and in some cases used, fossil fuels. Cave dwellers used coal for heat. Alexander the Great burned petroleum to scare the elephants, which were used in war, of his enemies. The Egyptians used asphalt, a derivative of petroleum, to preserve human remains. Some of the ancient peoples of Greece, Persia, and India worshipped the "eternal flames" created when lightning ignited natural gas that was seeping through cracks in the earth. The Chinese piped gas from shallow wells and burned it under large pans to evaporate sea water into salt.

The solid form of fossil fuel—coal—provided energy for many of our first industrial inventions. Coal provided fuel for steam engines in the late eighteenth century and it was used to produce "town gas" for gas lights in many cities. With the development of electric power in the late nineteenth century, coal's future became closely tied to electricity generation. Most electricity in the world today is still produced from coal. In the United States, 49 percent of electricity is produced from coal and China burns three times as much coal as the entire North American continent. However, coal is not the most widely used fossil fuel.

In the 1960s, petroleum overtook coal as the most widely used fossil fuel and the largest source of energy in the world. The thick oil, known as "black gold," provides the gasoline that fuels the world's hundreds of millions of cars. It also provides diesel fuel for the trucking industry and jet fuel for the world's airplanes. However, petroleum provides more than just fuel. Hundreds of important products are made from petroleum, such as plastics, lubricants, paints, and medicines.

Natural gas is the lightest of the fossil fuels. It was first used in America to illuminate the streets of Baltimore in 1816. The Fredonia Gas Light Company, founded in 1858, was the first natural gas company in the United States. Today, natural gas accounts for about a quarter of the energy we use. Natural gas is used primarily to provide heat for homes, businesses, and manufacturing processes and to produce electricity. But, like petroleum, a myriad of other products are produced from it. Industry is the biggest consumer of natural gas, using it as an ingredient in fertilizer, photographic film, ink, glue, paint, plastics, laundry detergent, and insect repellent.

Fossil fuels are called non-renewable energy sources because the earth contains a finite amount of these fuels. It required hundreds of millions of years for nature to produce coal, oil, and natural gas and we don't know how to speed the process. According to some estimates, the world will run out of coal sometime in the twenty-third or twenty-fourth century. These same estimates predict that the world will run out of natural gas and oil during the twenty-first century.

Many people believe that the United States should "decarbonize" its economy. They believe that using coal to produce electricity, using natural gas to heat our homes, and using gasoline to power our vehicles emits harmful amounts of carbon dioxide into the atmosphere, which causes global warming. Others say that the security of the nation is at risk if we continue to base our economy on oil imported from unstable regions of the world. Still others say that since fossil fuel supplies are finite, we should look to reducing their use: as they become scarcer, energy prices will skyrocket.

However, there are other people who think that the carbon economy will always exist. They believe the earth's climate may be changing, but not as much from emissions of carbon dioxide during energy consumption as from natural cyclical processes. Many people also believe that the United States can turn its abundant coal reserves—the United States is second only to China in coal production—into a liquid fuel to power automobiles, trucks, and planes for many years to come. Advanced technology already exists to turn coal into a type of synthetic oil. Still others say that electric cars—dependent on the electric grid and coal-fired electricity—will transport future Americans.

To what extent the future U.S. economy will depend on carbon is just one of the many energy debates that have the attention of Americans in the twenty-first century. As concerns about climate change intensify, as oil and gas reserves decline, and as energy prices rise, Americans are also discussing renewable energy's role in the twenty-first century and beyond. In *Opposing Viewpoints: Renewable Energy*, the contributors debate the many issues of renewable energy in the following chapters: What Is Renewable Energy? Is Renewable Energy Beneficial? What Are the Benefits of Ethanol as a Renewable Transportation Fuel? and How Should the Government Promote Renewable Energy and Fuels?

OPPOSING
VIEWPOINTS®
SERIES

CHAPTER 1

What Is Renewable Energy?

Chapter Preface

During the 2008 presidential campaign, many candidates talked about energy. Some of them talked about renewable energy, while others talked about alternative energy. "Renewable energy" and "alternative energy" are terms used to describe a variety of automotive and electricity-generating technologies that are different from those of conventional energy production.

Conventional electricity generation and automobile technology have not changed much in the last hundred years. They use age-old combustion techniques that burn fossil fuels. Most electricity is made today the same way it was more than a hundred years ago. Typically coal, natural gas, or oil are burned, and the heat is used to turn water into steam. The hot steam spins a magnet around copper wires. The process creates a magnetic field that electrifies the wire and produces an electric current. The vast majority of automobiles and trucks on the road today are propelled using an internal combustion engine fueled with fossil fuel-derived gasoline or diesel, the same type of engine and the same types of fuels that propelled the Model T at the beginning of the twentieth century.

When fossil fuel supplies become tight or when environmental or health problems caused by fossil fuel burning are in the spotlight, policy makers talk about changing the energy paradigm from conventional fossil fuel technologies to renewable or alternative energy. The term *renewable energy* entered the vocabulary of the American public during the 1970s. In October 1973, some of the Arab members of the Organization of Petroleum Exporting Countries (OPEC) stopped exporting oil to countries that supported Israel in the Yom Kippur War, the 1973 conflict between Israel and a coalition of Arab states, primarily Egypt and Syria. U.S. imports of oil from Arab countries dropped precipitously as a result. The oil crisis of 1973 inflicted serious pain on America. People were restricted to purchasing gasoline on certain days. Drivers of vehicles with odd-numbered license plates were allowed to purchase gasoline for their cars only on odd-numbered days of the month, while drivers of vehicles with even-numbered plates were allowed to purchase fuel only on even-numbered days. Those who experienced the 1973 OPEC oil embargo remember long lines at the gas pump and high gasoline prices. The 1970s energy crisis also led to conservation efforts. Americans were told to turn down thermostats and turn off the lights when leaving a room. It also led to a greater interest in renewable energy sources among members of government, the corporate sector, and the general public.

Most commonly, renewable energy refers to the electricity-generating sources of wind power, photovoltaic (i.e., solar) power, hydroelectric power, geothermal power, and biomass-fueled power. Solar, wind, hydroelectric, and geothermal systems capture energy from natural, infinitely renewable processes—sunlight, wind, moving water, and heat from beneath the earth—without the use of fossil fuels. Therefore, these energy sources emit no carbon dioxide and generally do not contribute to global warming. Most people do not dispute that solar, wind, hydroelectric, and geothermal systems are renewable, although in some cases there is debate about their environmental impacts.

There is a great deal of debate about what kinds of biomass energy sources are renewable. Energy can be derived from biomass in many different ways. Biomass refers to plants; trees; agricultural, food-processing, and wood-products waste; landfill gas; and sometimes "municipal solid waste," or garbage. Biomass can be used directly as a fuel and burned to create electricity. This occurs at what are called waste-to-energy facilities. Biomass can also be converted into gaseous or liquid fuels by certain types of bacteria. Biogas generated at landfills is a biomass-derived fuel that can be used to create electricity or burned for heating purposes. Ethanol and biodiesel are types of biogas, and are renewable transportation fuels that can be used in autos and trucks. Unlike solar, wind, hydroelectric, and geothermal power, biomass generally does have air emissions.

Alternative energy is an umbrella term that refers to anything other than conventional fuels and technologies. The term alternative energy entered the American vernacular during the 1990s as climate change concerns began surfacing. Many people started looking to less carbon-intensive ways of generating electricity or propelling vehicles. The term "alternative energy" is broader than renewable energy. It includes renewable energy and renewable fuels as well as advanced electricity-generating and vehicle technologies.

The most talked-about alternative energy technology is the hydrogen fuel cell. The fuel cell is very much like a battery. It contains a positive (cathode) and negative (anode) electrode where chemical reactions occur in the hydrogen fuel. However, unlike batteries, hydrogen fuel cells never "go dead." As long as they are supplied with hydrogen they continue operating and generating energy. Hydrogen fuel cells do not have any emissions, except water. Therefore, they do not contribute to climate change. Hydrogen fuel cells are versatile. They can be used to generate electricity and to propel automobiles and trucks. Some people envision a day when most of the cars on the road will be vehicles powered by fuel cells. Fuel cells, like many other alternative technologies, are not as commercially developed as renewable technologies. In some cases, the full-scale adoption of alternative energy technologies would require fundamental changes in the nation's energy infrastructure. For instance, before fuel cell vehicles can begin replacing gasoline-powered vehicles, the nation must develop a whole new infrastructure to distribute hydrogen fuel.

In addition to the technologies mentioned above, there are many others that may be considered renewable or alternative energy technologies. For instance, some people consider nuclear power a renewable fuel because advanced technologies have been developed that can recycle and reuse uranium fuels for an indefinite period of time. Other people consider power plants that generate electricity using "clean coal technologies," such as "integrated gasification combined cycle," or IGCC, an alternative technology. Although IGCC plants use coal, it is not burned, it is "gasified." As such, IGCC and other clean coal technologies are cleaner and more efficient than conventional coal-fired power plants.

What is and what is not considered renewable or alternative energy is subject to debate. All sources of energy, including renewable and alternative energy, have positive and negative attributes, environmentally and otherwise. People may weigh an energy source's positive and negative qualities differently and this impacts how they define renewable or alternative energy. In the following chapter, scientists, environmentalists, columnists, and research organizations provide their viewpoints on why particular energy sources should or should not be included within the definition of "renewable energy."

> *"Renewable energy utilizes natural cycles and systems—such as sunlight, wind, tides, and geothermal heat—to harness natural energy."*

Renewable Energy: An Overview

Environmental Literacy Council

In the following viewpoint, the Environmental Literacy Council (ELC) argues that renewable energy sources—wind, solar, hydropower, geothermal, and biomass—can help fight climate change because they generally have fewer greenhouse gas emissions than fossil fuels. However, renewable energy sources do have some associated pollution and currently they are expensive. The ELC says further investment in research and development is needed to promote renewable energy. The Environmental Literary Council is a nonprofit organization that provides educational tools and resources on environmental issues.

As you read, consider the following questions:

1. According to the Environmental Literacy Council (ELC), what is the largest source of energy at the present time?

2. Which two renewable energy sources does the ELC say are intermittent?

3. According to the ELC, what is the main obstacle to using renewable energy sources?

There are many different types of renewable energy sources, including biomass, wind, solar, hydropower, and geothermal heat. Many of these sources have a long history of use, with one of the oldest forms, wood, having been used for heating and cooking by early [humans]. Biomass [e.g., wood, among other things] is still the largest renewable energy resource used today.

Renewable sources of energy dominated up until the 20th century when fossil fuels became the preferred source due to their low cost and convenience. While fossil fuels remain the largest source of energy, concern over climate change, the rising cost of oil, and questions regarding fossil fuel supplies have increased interest in the production and use of renewable energy sources.

Renewable Energy Is Replenishable and Climate Friendly

Renewable energy utilizes natural cycles and systems—such as sunlight, wind, tides, and geothermal heat—to harness natural energy and create energy in a form ready for human consumption. Renewable energy sources differ from fossil fuels in that they can be replenished and their use produces little—if any—greenhouse gas [carbon dioxide]. Although most renewable energy sources do not produce greenhouse gases during energy production, they can consume a large amount of energy during their. . .construction and initial set-up. For example, it can take a wind turbine nearly 7 months of producing energy in order to offset its initial energy consumption and emission of greenhouse gases during its build. However, a

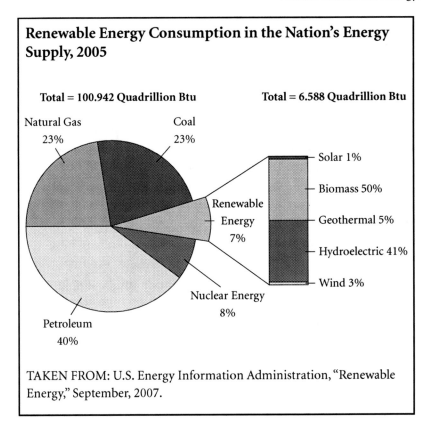

Renewable Energy Consumption in the Nation's Energy Supply, 2005

Total = 100.942 Quadrillion Btu   Total = 6.588 Quadrillion Btu

Natural Gas 23%

Coal 23%

Petroleum 40%

Nuclear Energy 8%

Renewable Energy 7%

Solar 1%

Biomass 50%

Geothermal 5%

Hydroelectric 41%

Wind 3%

TAKEN FROM: U.S. Energy Information Administration, "Renewable Energy," September, 2007.

wind turbine can typically produce over 30 times this amount of energy over the course of its lifetime. Therefore, although there are initial emissions in energy input, there is a net energy gain and greenhouse gas emission reduction from use.

Although relying solely on renewable energy would produce little greenhouse gas emissions, it is rarely feasible to do so. Some sources can be intermittent, such as solar and wind, requiring either use of a combination of energy sources or a form of energy storage. If the electric grid within the United States was powered only by renewable energy today, it would not be reliable. However, it is possible that with more research and development, renewable energy can become more reliable on a large scale basis.

Renewable Energy Combined with Fossil Fuels Is Optimal

The combination of fossil fuels and renewable energy has proven very successful—both at providing reliable power and at reducing overall greenhouse gas emissions. Biodiesel and ethanol, for example, can be combined with gasoline for cleaner transportation fuel. Sunlight can be combined with standard electric lighting to produce hybrid solar lighting, one of the newest developments in solar technology. Hydroelectric and wind power, used in conjunction with fossil fuels to produce electricity, can also reduce the amount of coal, natural gas and petroleum needed.

China and Germany currently have the largest investment in renewable energy technologies, although the fastest growing group of countries in terms of usage is in Europe, where governments promote renewable energy industries through tax incentives and subsidies. A number of countries have also developed renewable electricity standards, also known as renewable portfolio standards, which require electric service providers to gradually increase the amount of renewable energy sources used in their electricity supplies. In the U.S., nearly half the states and the District of Columbia have already developed such standards. Other countries include Australia, Japan, China, Italy, and the U.K. [United Kingdom].

Renewable Energy Obstacles and Criticisms

The main obstacle to using renewable energy sources is cost. While overall costs continue to decrease, most of the technologies remain more expensive than conventional fossil fuel technologies. However, much of the high cost stemming from renewable technologies is in the initial set-up, after which, operating costs tend to be lower than that of fossil fuel power plants. Some experts have suggested that if some of the costs associated with renewable energy were temporarily subsidized, it would help increase their production and capacity to produce energy.

While renewable energy technologies tend to be better for the environment, they also face additional criticisms. Although the majority of renewable energy sources do not directly emit pollution, the use of some materials in the production of renewable technologies, such as photovoltaic cells, generates both waste and pollution. Other sources require a large amount of land (harvesting for biomass, siting for wind or hydropower), which could be used for agricultural or other purposes, or left undeveloped. Hydro and wind power facilities can also have a negative impact on ecosystems, obstructing fish passage and bird migration, respectively.

Further investment in research and development is needed in order to continue to bring costs down and streamline renewable energy technologies to reduce their impact on the environment. However, renewable energy resources hold great potential for reducing the threat of climate change through decreased greenhouse gas emissions and, due to the fact that they can be replenished, could help alleviate the risk of exhausting the world's fossil fuel supply.

> *"I don't think there's anything cynical about it. Nuclear power is a 'renewable.'"*

Nuclear Power Is Renewable

Gia Milinovich

In the following viewpoint, Gia Milinovich argues that natural sources of renewable energy like the sun and the wind cannot provide enough energy for the entire world. If we depend on natural sources we will have to conserve energy, a concept Milinovich says is antithetical to human nature. She defends nuclear power as a renewable and scientifically based answer to the world's energy challenges. Gia Milinovich is a London-based science and technology broadcaster and blogger.

As you read, consider the following questions:

1. What does Milinovich believe is halted when we conserve energy?
2. What is the Climate Change Levy?
3. According to physics professor Bernard Cohen's calculations, how many years of energy are available from nuclear breeder reactors?

Gia Milinovich, "Nuclear Power Is a Renewable," *Potential Energy*, June 19, 2006. http://potentialenergyuk.com. Reproduced by permission of the Institute of Physics.

Carbon dioxide. Greenhouse gases. Pollution.

I don't think anyone believes that we should increase our emissions of any of these. . .and they are used by both sides to discredit the desirability of the "other" solution.

"Building a nuclear power plant/building a wind farm will produce XX tonnes of carbon. See? See? It's not carbon-neutral. Nyah!"

Like it or not, the fact is that pro-nuclear and anti-nuclear people are on the same side. Both sides want cleaner, long-term energy production in order to halt the Greenhouse Effect and to ensure a sustainable future. The 'rift' between the two comes about because one side wants to use "Science", [and] the other wants to use "Nature" in order to achieve this.

Natural Energy Production

Using Nature involves using the 'natural' sources of energy production which have been used since the dawn of civilisation—the sun, wind and water. In order to actually provide enough energy for the 6 billion people on the planet, using 'Nature' would also involve 'energy conservation'.

The traditionally 'Green' ethos has been: in order to 'conserve nature', we need to 'conserve energy', the implication being that 'Energy' destroys 'Nature'. We're told we all need to 'do our bit'—recycle and reuse, turn off the lights when they aren't being used, boil only enough water for the number of cups of tea you are drinking, not leaving your telly [television] on stand-by. We all know exactly what we're supposed to do by now. Many of us have been doing those things for years, most of the people in the world, however, haven't been doing any of these things. At all.

Most of the people in the world are in developing nations and, well, they want to have the kind of comfortable lifestyle we enjoy in the West. That's completely understandable. But it

2005 Energy Bill Promotes Nuclear Power

A controversial subject is nuclear power. You might remember, we've had a time in our country where people liked nuclear power, thought it was a strong solution to energy independence, and then we just shut her down because of engineering concerns. I strongly believe that if we want to keep this country competitive, if we want to make sure we can compete globally, we must promote civilian nuclear power. We must have more energy coming from nuclear power. . . .

Nuclear power is renewable, and there are no greenhouse gases associated with nuclear power. One of the problems we've had is that nobody wants to build any plants. They're afraid of the costs of regulation and the. . .[potential law suits] surrounding the construction of the nuclear power plants.

And so, in the energy bill I signed, the Congress wisely provided incentives and risk insurance for nuclear power plant construction. Last year only three companies were seeking to build power plants—nuclear power plants. Today 14 have expressed new interest in construction. In other words, there's a new industry beginning to come back.

George W. Bush, "President Bush Discusses Energy at Renewable Energy Conference," October 12, 2006. www.whitehouse.gov.

also takes 'energy' to achieve. The problem with 'conserving energy' is that it halts 'progress'.

"Scientific" Energy Production

Using science for energy production on the whole involves . . .nuclear fission or, in the future, nuclear fusion. We don't need to rely on everyone 'doing their bit' as we potentially have "an infinite source of uranium" even without the development of more efficient fusion reactors.

Recently there has been a move to 'reclassify' nuclear as a renewable—some cynically believe this is in order for the nuclear industry to be exempted from the Climate Change Levy—an environmental tax aimed at helping the UK [United Kingdom] reduce greenhouse gas emissions.

I don't think there's anything cynical about it. Nuclear power *is* a 'renewable'. If we use [physics professor] Bernard Cohen's calculations, we find we have 5 billion years of energy available using breeder reactors [nuclear reactors that produce more radioactive fuel than they consume]. Considering the sun is halfway through its lifetime of 10 billion years (give or take several million), then we have enough energy to last as long as the sun is able to support life. Even if we only had enough uranium to last us 5,000 years using current energy production technologies, I'd feel pretty confident that we'd have enough time to develop something new to take its place.

"Saving" Energy Is Not a Long Term Solution

I propose that 'energy conservation' goes against everything it means to be 'Human'. Of course, one has to accept the definition of being 'Human' as having an indefatigable desire to "explore" both our physical and intellectual worlds. To stop ourselves from exploring—our thoughts, our ideas, our dreams, our world, our solar system, our universe—risks our future *more* than polluting our planet ever could.

If Columbus or even John F. Kennedy had decided that 'energy conservation' was more important than 'exploration', where the hell would we be today?

"Oh, you know, I think it would be a bit 'wasteful' to find out if we can sail West or not. Let's just stay home and have a cup of. . .I'm not sure exactly *what* we could have as we've run out of tea because it just takes too darn long to get to China overland. . .but I'm sure we'll think of something."

"Go to the Moon? Nah. I think we should use our resources to work out how to recycle plastic. That's *really* sexy."

Investing in advanced technologies creates far more money than is spent. Queen Isabella and Spain reaped untold fortunes from her investment into Columbus' journeys. All mankind has continued to benefit from the scientific and technological knowledge gained from six moon landings. Why does anyone in their right mind believe that scrimping and saving our energy is a 'long term' solution?

Taking the "Scientific" Route Is Best

If we look at nuclear power as our first step to becoming a space-faring species (I mean, we're not going to get to Mars using hydro-electric power, are we?), then to me the idea of spending time and money on developing and building wind farms seems ludicrous. Almost as ridiculous as someone in the 19th century saying that we shouldn't develop steam engines for industry and should instead make more efficient water wheels. Actually, *not* 'almost', it's *more* ridiculous than that because we have the advantage of hindsight, [and] we can see *very* clearly that, throughout history, taking the 'Science' route has advanced civilisation time and time again. And that believing in [the] power, beauty or perfection of 'Nature', that 'Nature' knows best, has only ever hindered our development.

| *"Nuclear energy is no more a renewable
| energy source than oil or gas."*

Nuclear Power Is Not Renewable

Pembina Institute

In the following viewpoint, the Pembina Institute argues that nuclear energy is neither sustainable nor renewable, and that using nuclear power to offset greenhouse gas emissions and mitigate climate change is misguided. The institute claims that nuclear power is not renewable because uranium supplies are limited, and that while the greenhouse gas emissions from nuclear energy are an improvement over fossil fuel emissions, other sources, such as wind, solar, or hydroelectric energy, are better yet. The institute recommends several options other than nuclear energy to reduce greenhouse gas emissions. The Pembina Institute is a Canadian organization that promotes sustainable energy.

As you read, consider the following questions:

1. According to the Pembina Institute, how many radioactive waste fuel bundles are produced each year in Canada?

2. How much have world uranium prices increased since 2001, according to the Pembina Institute?

3. According to the institute, what environmental hazards resulted from nuclear reactor shutdowns in Ontario during the period 1996–2006?

The Pembina Institute thinks it's time to get clear about the real facts on nuclear power. The institute has taken a comprehensive look at the full spectrum of waste and pollution issues associated with all four major stages of nuclear energy production in Canada: uranium mining and milling; uranium refining, conversion and fuel fabrication; nuclear power plant operation; and waste fuel management.

Any cradle-to-grave analysis of an energy source is likely to find environmental and health impacts. However, the range and scale of impacts and risks associated with nuclear power production make it unique among energy sources.

Simply put, no other energy source combines the generation of a range of conventional pollutants and waste streams—including heavy metals, smog and acid rain contributors, and water contaminants—with the generation of extremely large volumes of radioactive wastes. Add to this accident, security and weapons proliferation risks that are not associated with any other energy source and this supposedly clean energy option looks a great deal dirtier and riskier.

Nuclear Power Is Not Clean

The nuclear power process leads to the release of hazardous and/or radioactive pollutants to air, land and water and is also—despite claims to the contrary—a source of greenhouse gases. Nuclear power production in Canada produces approximately 85,000 highly radioactive waste fuel bundles each year along with 500,000 tonnes [a tonne, also called a metric ton, is 1,000 kilograms] or more of toxic and radioactive mine tailings (wastes left after uranium extraction).

Neither Nuclear nor Coal Are Renewable

The nuclear industry has been on an aggressive campaign to paint itself as the answer to climate change emissions mitigation. But as we all know, uranium is not renewable, is imported, and the waste from the process has thousands of years of storage requirements—and as the National Academy of Sciences reported, pooled nuclear storage sites are subject to terrorism. Coal, as well, has its challenges, as a new rule approved by [President George W. Bush's administration] allows companies to "blow off" mountaintops in West Virginia harming farmland and waterways. Coal wastes and slag are still a major problem, and our taxpayer dollars still pay for black and brown lung benefits to coal miners. . . .Neither coal nor nuclear can be considered renewable or clean, when compared to the emissions or wastes from energy efficiency and renewable energy technologies.

Scott Sklar, "Is Nuclear Energy Renewable Energy?"
Renewable Energy World.com Online,
October 15, 2006. www.renewableenergyworld.com.

In fact, each stage of the nuclear energy production process generates large volumes of uniquely hard-to-manage wastes—wastes that in many cases will require care not for hundreds, but for hundreds of thousands of years.

Currently, no approved long-term plans for the management of these wastes exist in Canada. Meanwhile, the history of failures in storage facilities for uranium mine tailings in Canada and elsewhere demonstrates the problems these waste streams can lead to, including severe contamination of surface water and groundwater with radioactive and conventionally toxic pollutants.

Nuclear Power Is Not Sustainable

Nuclear energy is no more a renewable energy source than oil or gas. It relies on a non-renewable and now declining fuel supply—uranium. World uranium prices have increased more than tenfold since 2001, reflecting a worldwide uranium shortage. It is estimated that current Canadian reserves of high-grade uranium will last 40 years at current levels of consumption (compared to estimated natural gas reserves of approximately 70 years).

If we are forced to turn to lower-grade uranium deposits in the future, the already substantial emissions (including greenhouse gas emissions) from uranium mining and milling operations will increase, as will the amounts of waste rock and tailings generated by uranium mines and mills.

Nuclear proponents suggest that reprocessing waste fuel could be a way of dealing with both shrinking quantities of high-grade ores and the question of what to do with growing stockpiles of highly radioactive waste fuel. Reprocessing, however, has major waste and security risks of its own and would require the construction of extensive and expensive reprocessing facilities.

Fast breeder reactors [reactors that produce more radioactive fuel than they consume] that would create a near perpetual uranium-plutonium fuel cycle pose similar challenges and are thought to be decades away from even a prototype stage of development. Ideas like extracting uranium from seawater or using thorium as fuel in reactors are even less developed.

Nuclear Power Contributes to Climate Change

Greenhouse gases (GHG) are released at each stage of the nuclear power production process. Power plant construction is generally accepted as the most significant source of direct releases. Further releases of GHGs occur through the operation of equipment in the uranium mining process, the milling of uranium ore, mill tailings management activities, and refining and conversion operations. Significant releases of GHGs may also occur in the processes of plant refurbishment and decommissioning, the management of waste fuel and other radioactive wastes, and the decommissioning and remediation of uranium mine sites.

Overall, while the GHG emission profile of nuclear power looks attractive when compared with conventional fossil fuel sources, it is also clear that it is far from zero. At the same time nuclear power's GHG emission profile is generally higher that that of low-impact renewable energy sources like wind and run of the river hydro. A world wide shift to using nuclear power as a response to climate change would place pressure on high grade uranium ore reserves. The greenhouse gas emissions associated with nuclear would rise if greater use is made of lower grade ores, due to the need to extract and process more ore to produce the same amount of uranium for use as fuel in nuclear reactors.

It is not simply the direct GHG emissions from nuclear plants, however, that we have to consider when examining the usefulness of nuclear power as a climate change solution. In Ontario, the poor performance of nuclear units. . .has led to a dramatic increase in reliance on carbon-intensive coal power. The need to replace the power from the eight reactors shut down for repairs in 1997 meant that emissions of GHGs and sulphur dioxide from the province's coal-fired power plants more than doubled, while nitrogen oxide emissions increased by 170%. In fact there was a 120 megatonne increase in GHG emissions from the province's electricity generators due to reactor failures in the 1996–2006 period. . . .

The Big Picture

Turning to nuclear power to address climate change would mean trading the problem of greenhouse gas emissions, for which a wide range of other solutions exist, for several complex and difficult problems for which solutions are generally much more costly and difficult—if they exist at all. . . .

Proponents of nuclear energy often present the situation as a choice between expanding the role of nuclear power or risking blackouts and continuing on a business-as-usual path towards increasing GHG emissions and global climate change. The reality is that we have a wide range of options for keeping the lights on while significantly reducing GHG emissions without having to resort to the high cost and high-risk nuclear path. A combination of energy efficiency improvements, fuel switching, low impact renewable energy sources, and high efficiency uses of natural gas can provide the foundation for a low GHG emission energy system. Those kinds of options should be the focus of GHG reduction strategies and future energy policies.

VIEWPOINT 4

| "The generation of electricity by means of WTE [waste-to-energy] provides greater environmental benefits than any other source of renewable energy."

Energy from Garbage
Is Renewable

Nickolas J. Themelis and Karsten Millrath

In the following viewpoint, Nickolas J. Themelis and Karsten Millrath argue that municipal solid waste (MSW), or garbage, should be recognized along with other forms of biomass as a renewable source of energy. Facilities that burn MSW and generate electricity provide several environmental benefits, say the authors. These facilities are much cleaner than coal-fired power plants, and using trash to generate electricity is better than dumping it in landfills. Nickolas J. Themelis is the director of the Earth Engineering Center at Columbia University. Karsten Millrath was a post doctoral research scientist at the Earth Engineering Center until 2005.

Nickolas J. Themelis and Karsten Millrath, "The Case for WTE as a Renewable Source of Energy" (12th North American Waste to Energy Conference), New York, NY: The Earth Engineering Center, Columbia University and Waste-to-Energy Research and Technology Council, 2004. Reproduced by permission.

As you read, consider the following questions:

1. What are some of the components of municipal solid waste that Themelis and Millrath discuss? Name three made from non-renewable fossil fuels.

2. According to Themelis and Millrath, since the 1990s waste-to-energy facilities have become one of the cleanest sources of energy as result of the implementation of what EPA regulations?

3. According to Themelis and Millrath, what is the recycling rate for communities with waste-to-energy facilities? What is it for communities without waste-to-energy facilities?

In the traditional sense, renewable sources of energy are those that nature can replenish, such as waterpower, windpower, solar radiation and biomass (wood and plant waste). However, the U.S. [United States] municipal solid wastes (MSW) contain a large fraction of paper, food wastes, cotton and leather, all of which are renewable materials under proper stewardship of the Earth. Municipal solid wastes also contain man-made plastics, rubber and fabrics that were produced using non-renewable fossil fuels. All these materials were produced because they were needed by humanity. Although it is desirable to minimize the amount of materials used per capita, and also the generation of wastes during production and distribution of goods, a certain quantity of wastes will always be generated. Therefore, if the produced waste is to be disposed in some way, there is a continuous new stream to replenish it. . . .

An Alternative to Landfilling

In the U.S. and universally, the dominant method of disposing the MSW stream has been landfilling. Developed nations that have a limited amount of land, such as Denmark, Holland and Japan, realized that landfilled putrescible [biodegradable] wastes turn the land into unusable space; therefore, alternative means were sought to reduce the MSW volume. Their first priority has been to reduce the generation of waste and then try to recover as much as possible of the materials contained in MSW. Their experience showed that while some materials could be recovered economically, there was a large remaining fraction that could either be used as a fuel or landfilled. The present generation of waste-to-energy [WTE] plants uses MSW as a fuel to generate electricity and recover ferrous [iron], and in some cases non-ferrous, materials from the ash.

Like other essential technologies, for example steelmaking, the WTE industry in the U.S. and abroad went through a long learning process in controlling the significant environmental problems associated with high-volume, high-temperature processes. However, since the 1990s, as a result of implementing the maximum available control technology (MACT) regulations of U.S. EPA [Environmental Protection Agency], the WTE industry in the U.S. has transformed itself from a major polluter to "one of the cleanest sources" of energy as recognized by the U.S. EPA....

At this time, the U.S. DOE [Department of Energy] categorizes WTE as one type of biomass, as shown in the following definition: *The term "biomass" means any plant derived organic matter available on a renewable basis, including dedicated energy crops and trees, agricultural food and feed crops, agricultural crop wastes and residues, wood wastes and residues, aquatic plants, animal wastes, municipal wastes, and other waste materials.*

Opposition to Calling WTE "Renewable"

A detailed review of the opposition to renewable energy status for WTE facilities in the U.S. has shown that there are five arguments repeated in a variety of statements:

1. There should be much less municipal solid waste generated and what is generated should be recycled. When

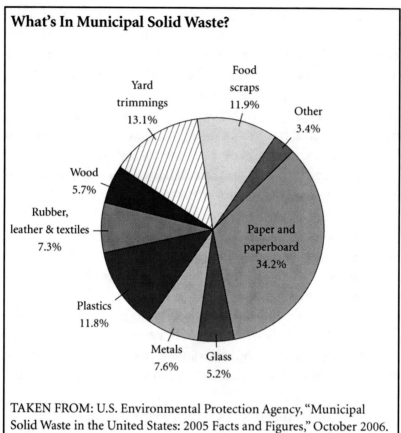

What's In Municipal Solid Waste?

Food scraps 11.9%

Yard trimmings 13.1%

Other 3.4%

Wood 5.7%

Rubber, leather & textiles 7.3%

Paper and paperboard 34.2%

Plastics 11.8%

Metals 7.6%

Glass 5.2%

TAKEN FROM: U.S. Environmental Protection Agency, "Municipal Solid Waste in the United States: 2005 Facts and Figures," October 2006.

this is done, there will not be waste fuel for waste-to-energy power plants in the future. Therefore, waste-to-energy is not a renewable source of energy.

2. Granting renewable status to waste-to-energy will inhibit efforts to recycle wastes.

3. In considering renewable energy status, waste-to-energy should not be credited with the avoided environmental impacts of landfilling.

4. Waste-to-energy is incineration and, on a per kWh [kilowatt hour of electricity] basis, the generation of electricity by waste-to-energy is more polluting than by coal-fired power plants.

5. Granting renewable energy status to waste-to-energy will lead to building new waste-to-energy facilities in low-income areas that are already suffering environmental injustice.

Opposition's Arguments Are Groundless

The reasoning behind these five arguments runs contrary to the known facts, both within New York State and the rest of the developed world. These facts are discussed below. . . .

The U.S. generated about 370 million tons of MSW in 2002. The nationwide recycling rate was 26.7%. The rest was either combusted in WTE plants (7.7%) or landfilled (65.6%) [according to a 2004 article in *Biocycle*]. It cannot be expected that the best possible practice of waste reduction and recycling will lead to the often-acclaimed "zero waste" scenario. . . .

Recycling and waste-to-energy are not competing but complementary and essential means of waste management. Waste-to-energy does not displace recycling; it displaces landfilling of trash. In fact, [studies have shown] the recycling rate for communities with WTE facilities was reported to be 33%, substantially higher than the average U.S. rate of 26.7%. At most WTE plants, materials such as ferrous metals are recovered from the waste stream either before or after combustion and thus, diverted from landfills.

The comparison of WTE to recycling, rather than to landfilling, is misleading to say the least: Obviously, WTE plants do not choose to combust recyclable materials. They have to process all the mixed trash that is delivered to them: plastic wastes, paper wastes, textile wastes, wood wastes, food wastes, disposable diapers and all other wastes. The 28.5 million short tons of municipal solid waste that are combusted annually in the U.S., as well as the hundreds of millions of tons landfilled, represent the real world of used materials that cannot be recycled. . . .

WTE Can Be Environmentally Friendly

Waste-to-energy is the only form of renewable energy that: a) reduces environmental impacts of fossil fuel use; and also, b) reduces the environmental impacts of the only other alternative for waste disposal, landfilling. Therefore, it is eminently fair to consider both of these advantages. The search for renewable energy sources is motivated by the desire to reduce use of fossil fuels. WTE facilities in the U.S. produce about 500 kWh per ton of municipal solid waste, thus obviating the use of either 0.3 tons of coal or 1 barrel of fuel oil per ton of MSW combusted. In addition, waste-to-energy reduces the need for landfilling by one ton of municipal solid waste per ton of trash combusted. Thus, the generation of electricity by means of WTE provides greater environmental benefits than any other source of renewable energy for the simple reason that in addition to the benefit of reducing the use of fossil fuels, as all other renewable energy sources do, it also avoids the environmental impacts of landfilling. . . .

There are nearly one hundred waste-to-energy power plants in the U.S. and more than 1600 incinerators. Incinerators were developed to control the spreading of diseases and limit the number of vectors that are attracted by waste. WTE facilities are the result of the technological evolution of incinerators over several decades and they [were] equipped after the implementation of the EPA-mandated Maximum Available Control Technology (MACT) regulations. . .[making them superior] to many coal-fired power plants in the U.S. Also, in contrast to coal-fired power plants, WTE serves two purposes, conserving non-renewable fossil fuels and also land for landfilling. . . .

WTE facilities, as well as any other industrial installations, should be built at locations where they will improve, rather than deteriorate, the quality of life of the surrounding community, in terms of esthetics, provision of jobs and services, and environmental quality. While it is very difficult to site new WTE facilities, there is growing public acceptance of already built WTE plants. . . .

Since WTE is environmentally better than landfilling and, in addition, it generates electricity thus reducing our dependence on fossil fuels, it should be included in the benefits to be provided to other sources of renewable energy.

> "If garbage were defined as a 'renewable
> energy resource,' garbage incinerators
> would naturally become an official part
> of the nation's renewable energy strat-
> egy. This will be good for incinerator
> companies but bad for everyone else."

Energy from Garbage Is Not Renewable

Peter Montague

*In the following viewpoint, Peter Montague asserts that munici-
pal solid waste, or garbage, is not renewable. He says that the
waste industry in the United States has mounted a campaign to
build "waste-to-energy" facilities in towns and cities across the
country. Montague suggests that what the waste industry calls
waste-to-energy, or waste gasification, facilities are really incinerators in disguise, and they are a losing proposition for local
communities and the entire nation. Calling facilities that convert
trash to energy "renewable" is misleading, since significant
amounts of energy will need to be consumed to recreate all of
the products that eventual end up in incinerators. Also, according to Montague, as the nation moves closer to a "zero waste"*

Peter Montague, "Incinerators Are Making A Comeback (Or Trying)," *Rachel's Democracy & Health News*, October 19, 2006. Available at www.precaution.org. Reproduced
by permission.

lifestyle, incinerators will become less viable. Peter Montague is the editor of Rachel's Democracy & Health, *a newsletter of the Environmental Research Foundation.*

As you read, consider the following questions:

1. According to Montague, what happens to the toxic residue that is created when garbage is heated?

2. What two forces are driving the resurgence of incinerator production and use in the U.S., according to Montague?

3. Why, specifically, does Montague conclude that burning garbage "wastes huge amounts of energy"?

Cheap waste disposal prevents us from making progress against pollution.

So long as waste disposal remains cheap, corporations and governments have little incentive to recycle, re-use, compost, or avoid making waste in the first place.

If disposal is cheap, there is no compelling reason to invest in green chemistry, clean production, alternative energy, green building, or cradle-to-cradle [sustainable, recyclable] manufacturing.

Cheap disposal = landfills and incinerators. Let's talk incinerators.

Incinerators Are Never Called Incinerators

Garbage incinerators are making a big comeback in the U.S.—or trying to. The City of Los Angeles, California is thinking about building seven of them. There may be as many as 40 (or more) proposed incinerators of one kind or another in Alaska, Hawaii, Puerto Rico and the lower 48. All of them promise to take mixed municipal waste and heat it up to reduce the volume of garbage and extract small amounts of useful energy in the process.

Heating mixed waste (garbage) creates toxic air emissions and the toxicant-containing residual—whether ash or a rock-like "clinker"—will be buried in the ground where it remains available forever, threatening groundwater.

These new incinerators are never called incinerators—they go by names like pyrolysis or gasification plants, or plasma arc melters, or simply "conversion" machines. But they all to heat mixed waste, extract some energy, and bury the leftovers in the ground.

Rarely does anyone ask, "How much energy will it take to start from scratch and re-create all the goods destroyed by the incinerator?" No one asks because the answer reveals that incinerators are huge energy-wasters, not energy-savers. As Monica Wilson of GAIA [Global Alliance for Incinerator Alternative] says (quoting [chemistry professor Paul Connett]), "Even if you could make an incinerator safe, you couldn't make one sensible."

Two things seem to be driving the incinerator resurgence:

(a) the recent glimmer of recognition in Washington that dependence on oil is a bad for the planet and especially bad for the U.S.; and

(b) a federal law that requires electric utilities to buy any electricity produced by incinerators.

Incinerators, Politics, and Money

For political reasons, incinerators have always been attractive to some local officials. Take [a 2006 proposal] in St. Petersburg, Florida, where Cecil D. Davis IV, [a candidate for] City Council, proposed to move 500 mostly black families out of their homes in South Brooksville to replace them with an incinerator, which he promised [would] be built in record time if he [got] elected. The up-front cost to taxpayers [would] be $500 million.

Local governments rarely get a chance to play around with a huge sum like $500 million of other people's money. All the

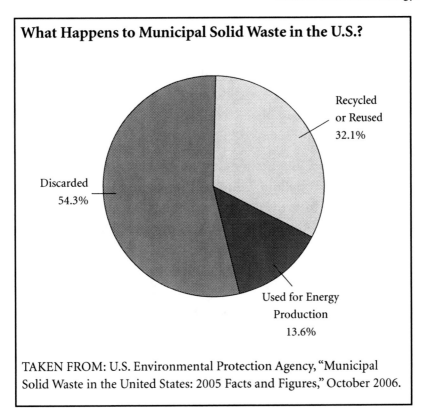

What Happens to Municipal Solid Waste in the U.S.?

Recycled or Reused 32.1%

Discarded 54.3%

Used for Energy Production 13.6%

TAKEN FROM: U.S. Environmental Protection Agency, "Municipal Solid Waste in the United States: 2005 Facts and Figures," October 2006.

political insiders get to scoop off their own little slice of this huge pie—lawyers, bankers, engineers, environmental consultants, construction firms, labor leaders, regulatory experts, realtors, lobbyist, and all manner of other hangers-on will get a chance to snag their own tenth-of-a-percent and make a bundle. (A tenth of a percent of $500 million is $500 thousand.)

Furthermore, all the money will be sloshing around during the short planning and construction phase. After the machine is built, and the profits have been taken, the builders and their friends can retire into the woodwork and disappear, leaving the taxpayer and future City Councils to deal with mounting problems for the next 30 years or more.

Problems with Incinerators Are Commonplace

And the problems are substantial. We searched a national database of newspapers for incinerator stories that were published during the first three weeks of October, 2006, and here are some of the problems being reported:

- In Akron, Ohio a company called Akron Thermal owes the city $5 million in unpaid sewer and water bills, $845,000 in unpaid rent, and $80,000 in unpaid franchise fees. Akron Thermal also owes the state of Ohio $3.2 million in unpaid excise taxes, and it owes Summit County about $300,000 in unpaid public utility personal property tax. Akron Thermal no longer burns garbage because the plant suffered a serious explosion in 1984, killing 3 workers, when a New Jersey firm sent some illegal garbage to the plant. A decade a later, a scam to avoid paying plant fees resulted in the arrest of a dozen waste haulers and plant employees, costing the city $500,000. Now the plant burns wood chips and low-sulphur coal because local businesses are dependent on the steam from the plant for heat.

- In Passaic County, New Jersey a waste hauler is suing the local utility authority for $3.5 million it says the county owes. The County says the finances of its incinerator are so shaky it can't afford to pay its debts. The situation developed after the U.S. Supreme Court declared that New Jersey waste producers could ship their wastes out of county (indeed, out of state) instead of sending them to the expensive Passaic incinerator. This legal decision in 1997 threw the incinerator's business plan into a cocked hat. Anyone thinking about building an incinerator today should think twice—changing laws and regulations can cause bankruptcy overnight.

- Biddeford, Maine has spent over two years negotiating with the Maine Energy Recovery Company, trying to settle lawsuits, disputes over tax abatements, and disagreements over the assessed value of the incinerator. Residents of Biddeford have complained about odors from the plant since it opened in 1987. Reportedly the new agreement between Biddeford and the incinerator operator imposes financial penalties on the city if it ever sues the incinerator operator, and opens the incinerator to a new class of waste—construction and demolition debris. In other locales, constructon and demolition debris is being recycled and re-used, not destroyed by incineration. Suits between incinerator companies and governments are common, so Biddeford may be getting itself into a weak position by agreeing to pay penalties if it ever has to sue.

- In Georgia, politics has raised its venal head in the state legislature, where the waste industry is lobbying to gut the state's sunshine [disclosure] laws. A Republican proposal would cloak local economic development decisions—including the decision to build incinerators—in secrecy until after deal is done. Specifically, the proposed law "would allow unelected boards to provide incentives for companies to build incinerators, waste disposal sites or other job-creating businesses without having to disclose them publicly until after the deal had been negotiated," according to the *Atlanta Journal-Constitution*.

- In Peekskill, New York the city tried to charge waste haulers a special fee for damage and pollution caused by 3000 trucks per year delivering garbage to. . .[an] incinerator. The city claimed that the incinerator degraded city streets and dripped noxious pollution into the community from leaky, overfilled trucks. A judge struck down the Peekskill law as unconstitutional.

- The contribution of now-defunct incinerators to soil and water contamination is the subject of specific, multi-million dollar investigations in Connecticut, Pennsylvania, Florida, California, and Ohio. And remember, this is just a review of news stories during a one-month period, October, 2006. . . .

- Federal oversight of incinerators is reportedly less than thorough—even in the case of the most dangerous machines, those that burn hazardous wastes. After the Sierra Club and the American Bottom Conservancy sued to force EPA [U.S. Environmental Protection Agency] to enforce the law, U.S. EPA demanded that the Onyx Incinerator in Sauget, Illinois apply for a permit to operate. Onyx operated for years without a permit. According to the *St. Louis Post-Dispatch*, the incinerator had been fined repeatedly by state authorities for uncontrolled releases, accidents, and fires.

- In Texas, the incinerator industry has lobbied for the past three legislative sessions to try to get municipal garbage defined as a "renewable energy source." So far the effort has failed, but it is crystal clear that this redefinition is a main strategy of the garbage industry.

Calling Incinerators Renewable Is Bad for Everyone

Think about that. If garbage were defined as a "renewable energy resource," garbage incinerators would naturally become an official part of the nation's renewable energy strategy. This will be good for incinerator companies but bad for everyone else.

Burning garbage wastes huge amounts of energy because everything destroyed in an incinerator must be re-created from scratch starting with the mining and logging of virgin materials, transportation, processing, more transportation, and manufacture—all accompanied by massive pollution and waste.

There can only be an endless supply of garbage if the U.S. maintains its wasteful lifestyle. When we get around to adopting a precautionary waste philosophy (zero waste), garbage will diminish dramatically. Incinerator companies that need garbage to feed their machines will oppose sensible solid waste policies by hook and by crook. We must therefore once again mount a serious campaign against them and their wasteful machines.

"As natural resources go, animal manure is abundant and endlessly renewable."

Manure Processed in Methane Digesters Is Renewable

Martha T. Moore

In the following viewpoint, Martha T. Moore discusses the environmental and economic benefits of methane digesters. Methane digesters use gas-generating microbes to convert animal manure into methane gas, which is then used to generate electricity. Digesters can help farmers save money on electric bills and make money by selling excess electricity to the power grid. According to Moore, the digesters also solve manure-related problems like odor and greenhouse gas emissions. "Cow power," or "poop power," says Moore, is abundant and renewable. Martha T. Moore is a journalist for USA Today.

As you read, consider the following questions:

1. According to Moore, why are more farmers becoming interested in methane digesters?

2. How many gallons of manure does a cow produce a day, according to Moore?

3. According to the U.S. Department of Energy, central
   Vermont's Cow Power program is one of about how
   many "green power" programs nationally?

Marie Audet's cows produce three things: milk, fertilizer
and electricity.

They earn only about $13 per hundred pounds for the
milk, a 25-year low, but 12 cents per kilowatt-hour for the
electricity, a 4-cent premium over the market price.

That's why the Audet family and a growing number of
other dairy farmers have decided there's money in manure.
Power derived from manure is changing from an alternative-
fuel experiment to a business, pushed by oil costs, low milk
prices and new laws restricting harmful gas emissions and requiring the use of renewable energy.

Cow Power

Two generators at the Audets' Blue Spruce Farm feed electricity to the local utility. They run on methane gas derived from
cow manure. The farm is part of Cow Power, a program of
the local electric company, Central Vermont Public Service.
Cow Power gives customers the option to pay higher rates to
subsidize farm-generated, poop-powered electricity. The 4-cent
premium the farmers are paid helps cover the cost of installing an anaerobic [using little or no oxygen] digester that ex-
tracts methane from cowpies.

Now, after two years as Cow Power pioneers, the Audets
are about to get company. [In January 2007] Mark and
Amanda St. Pierre, who run Pleasant Valley Farm a mile from
the Canadian border, will become the second dairy farmers in
Vermont to sell poop power. Four more Vermont farms are to
go online in [2007]. In California, six dairy farms have signed
up to pump manure-derived methane into the pipelines of
Pacific Gas and Electric.

Even proponents say methane digesters will never produce
more than a tiny fraction of the energy consumed in the USA,

Digesters Are Practical Way to Protect Environment

Virtually all major environmental groups support methane digesters as a practical way to reduce water pollution, air pollution and greenhouse gas emissions from farms. Digesters also kill disease-causing bacteria and mitigate odors.

The technology can be cost-effective for all types of dairies, large and small, organic and not, particularly when dairies can sell surplus electricity.

A recent study by the California Public Utilities Commission concluded that the environmental, economic and social benefits of methane digesters rank above other local sources of electricity, including solar. . . .

Methane digesters are a practical, cost-effective way to produce renewable energy and to protect the environment.

Allen Dusault, "Renewable Energy: Letter to the Editor,"
New York Times, *March 11, 2006. www.nytimes.com.*

even if all of the nation's 7,000 large dairy and hog farms installed them. But methane digesters can have a big effect on the economics of a dairy farm, the quality of life of its neighbors and on the pollutants a farm produces.

Digesters Solve Problems

As natural resources go, animal manure is abundant and endlessly renewable. Cows produce as much as 30 gallons a day, every day. "One thing for sure we can count on is a constant supply of it," Mark St. Pierre says.

Until now, the St. Pierres, like the Audets, stored manure in large open pits referred to as lagoons. Methane given off by the manure escaped into the air, contributing to the "greenhouse effect" blamed for global warming. The smell escaped, too, especially when manure was spread on fields as fertilizer.

Anaerobic digesters, also called methane digesters, solve both problems. Manure is swept from dairy barns by automated floor scrapers and goes down pipes into the digester, an insulated tank. The Vermont digesters are sunk most of the way into the ground.

The digester, which holds about three weeks' worth of manure, contains bacteria similar to those in a cow's stomach. The tank is heated and cooks the manure. The methane given off is piped away to fuel generators or flows directly to the utility's gas pipeline.

What remains is separated into liquid and a soft, odorless mulch like peat moss. The mulch is used as bedding for the cows instead of sawdust, saving the Audets, for example, $50,000 a year. The sawdust "was like gold," Audets says. With the "biosolids" from manure, she loves "having as much of that stuff as we want and making our cows comfortable." The Audets sell the extra as garden fertilizer.

The liquid is pumped into the old manure lagoons and then spread on fields as fertilizer, just as raw manure is on other farms. The thinner liquid soaks into the ground better than raw manure and minimizes runoff from fields into nearby Lake Champlain, Audet says. Perhaps the best part: It doesn't smell.

4 Cents Adds Up

Farmers in the Cow Power program still pay for the electricity they use on the farm. But they produce more that they use, and they sell what they produce to the electric company for 95% of the wholesale price plus 4 cents per kilowatt-hour. The St. Pierres calculate that they'll gross $200,000 a year on the sales.

"Their 4 cents is what makes it go, on paper," Amanda St. Pierre says. The extra income is "definitely going to be a factor in our being here in the next 10 years."

Last month, grain giant Cargill agreed to go into business with Environmental Power, a New Hampshire company that installs methane digesters on farms, sells the gas to utilities and pays the farmers a percentage. Cargill will connect the company with the huge number of farms it does business with.

"We have folks out there running around" talking to farmers about installing methane digesters, says Albert Morales, executive vice president of Environmental Power. "But when you're a farmer and Cargill shows up and says, 'We think you should do this,' it carries more weight."

Already, Environmental Power has installed digesters at three farms in Wisconsin that sell electricity to their local utility and is building more at a feedlot in Texas that will sell methane.

Digesters Part of "Green" Movement

In California, Pacific Gas and Electric [PG&E] agreed [in November 2006] to buy methane from six dairies where Environmental Power runs digesters. Pushing the utility is a new state law requiring power companies to buy 20% of their electricity from renewable sources by the year 2010. [In 2006], PG&E [got] 12% of its energy from renewable sources, including wind, geothermal energy and animal waste, according to spokeswoman Darlene Chiu. California has also passed legislation requiring the reduction of greenhouse-gas emissions.

Central Vermont's Cow Power program is one of about 600 "green power" programs nationally, according to the U.S. Department of Energy, in which consumers agree to pay a premium on their electric bills, knowing that the extra money supports renewable-energy programs like wind or solar power. It's the only one that relies entirely on cow manure.

About 2.4% of the utility's customers have signed up, well above the 1.3% average participation in green-power programs.

Vermont's open farm fields and the impressive views—Audet's cows have a view of the Adirondack Mountains and St. Pierre's can see the Green Mountains—are what Cow Power buyers went to preserve. The rural landscape "is a nonrenewable resource," Audet says. "That's why people want to pay the 4 cents."

*"A fuel that damages the environment is
not 'renewable.'"*

Manure Processed in Methane Digesters Should Not Be Considered Renewable

Sierra Club

In the following viewpoint, the Sierra Club makes a case against methane digesters and the large factory farms called "concentrated animal feeding operations," or CAFOs, which most often employ this energy-generating technology. The Sierra Club believes methane digesters do little to improve the environment and, worse, they enable CAFOs to thrive. The organization opposes CAFOs because they pollute the air and water and promote harmful farming practices. They oppose the inclusion of methane digesters under the renewable energy umbrella because they believe that manure-fueled digesters are inefficient, damaging to the environment, and helpful only to CAFOs. The Sierra Club is one of the nation's oldest nonprofit environmental protection organizations.

Sierra Club, "Sierra Club Guidance: Methane Digesters and Concentrated Animal Feeding Operation (CAFO) Waste," Sierra Club Mother Lode Chapter, October 20, 2004. Reproduced by permission.

As you read, consider the following questions:

1. What does anaerobic mean?

2. According to the Sierra Club, what two constituents of swine and poultry manure can pose problems when the solid waste is applied as fertilizer or soil conditioner?

3. According to the Sierra Club, a clean, renewable energy future must be built upon what three things?

The use of methane digesters to produce energy from animal manure may have a role in addressing environmental problems and meeting energy needs, but the Sierra Club opposes public subsidies to such energy generation at large concentrated animal feeding operations (CAFOs) because of the environmental and social damage associated with them: polluting our waters and our air; excessive use of antibiotics and hormones; mistreatment of animals; and harming rural communities and small farms.

Methane digesters are anaerobic (low or no oxygen) chambers which facilitate the breakdown of manure by anaerobic bacteria with the release of methane and other gases as a byproduct of their metabolism—ammonia, nitrogen, hydrogen sulfide, and sulfur dioxide. Methane can be burned directly in stoves or burners, to heat the digesters, and it can be converted to electricity. There are several different types of systems but all commercially available systems are expensive to install and require manure from a large numbers of animals to operate. . . .

CAFO Manure So Contaminated, Digesters Can Do Little to Help

CAFO waste streams are so large and contaminated that methane digesters mitigate only a small fraction of their environment damage. [According to the U.S. Environmental Protection Agency] equipment costs and maintenance for conversion to energy are high. The biogas must have ammonia, moisture, and particulate pollution (dust) removed, and then be compressed. It requires additional cleaning if it is to be sent into a natural gas pipeline.

Most environmental damage caused by CAFOs, however, remains unabated. Excess nutrients which run off from waste lagoons or land-applied waste residuals suffocate the life out of our waters. The volume of solid waste remaining is not significantly diminished and requires proper disposal. The solid waste is often land applied as "fertilizer" or "soil conditioner" but can pose problems because anaerobic digestion does not remove antibiotics and heavy metals passed by dosed swine and poultry. In addition, although pathogen numbers decrease, the decrease may be ephemeral as the pathogens regrow [according to one study]. Numerous studies have demonstrated that these toxic and pathogenic contaminants are entering the environment in substantial concentrations. Further, digesters pose a risk of explosion and create both nitrogenous and sulfurous gases which may be emitted. In sum, the potential for methane digesters to partially mitigate some of the extensive and pervasive damage caused by CAFOs does not justify the use of this technology as a basis to support the development of new CAFOs. Existing CAFOs may reduce the problems they are currently causing by use of methane digesters. However, they should be installed at the cost of the CAFO owner and not from public subsidy. . . .

Manure-Fueled Digesters Not Renewable

A fuel that damages the environment is not "renewable." The anaerobic decomposition of CAFO manure, like the decomposition of garbage in landfills, and waste-burning incinerators, is symptomatic of inefficient waste treatment, treatment necessitated by inefficient, wasteful industries, practices, and processes. The Sierra Club favors conservation of materials and energy, energy efficiency in processes and operations, and the recycling of materials over the thermal destruction of ma-

Manure Is Brown Not Green

Talk of reducing our dependence on foreign oil through alternative energy sources like biomass is everywhere these days—even on [President George W. Bush's] lips. As a livestock farmer and environmental lawyer, I've paid particular attention to discussion about using manure as "green power." The idea sounds appealing, but power from manure turns out to be a poor source of energy. Unlike solar or wind, it can create more environmental problems than it solves. And it ends up subsidizing large agribusiness. That's why energy from manure should really be considered a form of "brown power."

Nicolette Hahn Niman, "A Load of Manure," New York Times, *March 4, 2006. www.nytimes.com.*

terials for their energy content. Small farms which utilize land sufficient to support the number of animals being raised can be operated so that the land, air, and water are not degraded and the waste can be recycled into the soil rather than accumulating and decomposing via the methane-generating anaerobic process. CAFO waste lagoons and landfills release heat, a waste of thermal energy and methane, a waste of chemical energy. Capturing energy from these processes reduces some of the environmental damage associated with these wasteful and inefficient systems but it doesn't move us towards a clean, renewable energy future which must be built upon conservation, efficiency, and material recycling.

Subsidies for energy production from digesters have become a frequent provision in energy legislation. Some fossil fuel use may be displaced by methane digesters but it is a small amount. Similarly, some global warming gas emissions are reduced by the use of digesters but CAFOs are a minor contributor overall [according to the EPA]. The benefits of methane digesters in terms of energy policy are small so subsidies for CAFO digesters are not consistent with good energy policy. The fuel for digesters is primarily CAFO manure, a waste which depletes and degrades natural resources. In evaluating whether a subsidy under consideration might be supportable, one must consider whether the subsidy would produce greater environmental gains if applied, for instance, to a clean, renewable energy source.

Taking a Broader Perspective

For forward-thinking energy policy, we have to take a broader perspective. A public subsidy of $200,000 in public money could provide about 50% of the funding necessary for a digester which could collect the methane generated by the water-flushed manure of 1,000 dairy cows, methane which would be burned for energy and would emit pollutants into the atmosphere. That same funding could pay for the installation of wind turbines which would supplant fossil fuel burning on that same farm without emitting air pollutants. That same funding could subsidize smaller dairy farms which generate dry manure rather than water-flushed manure; dry manure generates only minimal amounts of methane. As citizens, it is our responsibility to "do the math" and to ensure that we are looking towards long-term solutions, not just short-term fixes.

Many states are now considering legislation which promotes renewable energy and includes methane digesters as a potential source for such energy. The Sierra Club prefers clean, renewable energy sources over CAFO waste so legislation should be evaluated to ensure that support for clean renewable fuels is strong. We also want to ensure that when methane digester energy is included in legislation, its impacts are adequately regulated and small farms are provided with fair access to the technology and to the energy grids which permit the sale of the energy. Smaller farms may require additional access and provisions to allow them effective and fair access.

The Sierra Club opposes the development of new CAFOs, and, therefore opposes new CAFOs with methane digesters because the problems of CAFOs will greatly outweigh the potential benefits of methane digesters.... Local, state, and federal environmental laws should be in place to protect public health and the environment from the impacts of CAFOs. Existing CAFO owners must comply with all these laws and must have invested in the technologies needed to eliminate all forms of pollution.

Periodical Bibliography

The following articles have been selected to supplement the diverse views presented in this chapter.

Michael Behar — "The Prophet of Garbage," *PopSci.com.* March 1, 2007.

Daniela Chen — "Converting Trash Gas into Energy Gold," *CNN.com.* July 17, 2006.

The Economist — "The Atom and the Windmill: Energy Sources," October 27, 2007.

Ed Hiserodt — "The 'Other' Renewables," *The New American.* November 12, 2007.

Michael Hoexter — "The Renewable Electron Economy Part IX: What Is Renewable Energy Anyway?," *Green Thoughts.* December 9, 2007. http://terra verde.wordpress.com.

Arjun Makhijani — "Nuclear Power, Not Renewable Energy Is Risky Course for U.S.," *Desert Morning News.* February 10, 2008.

Jim Montavilli — "The Clean Energy Path: Renewable Options," *E: The Environmental Magazine.* July–August 2007.

Nick Schulz — "Hot Rocks, Cool Technology," *The American.* May–June 2007.

ScienceDaily — "Sound Way to Turn Heat into Electricity," June 4, 2007.

Andrew Welsh-Huggins — "Governors: Include Coal in Energy Debate," *Huffington Post.* February 23, 2008. www.huffingtonpost.com.

Jeremy Wilcox — "Nuclear Is Not an Energy Panacea, Nor Are Renewables," *Modern Power Systems.* February 2008.

OPPOSING
VIEWPOINTS®
SERIES

CHAPTER 2

Is Renewable Energy Beneficial?

Chapter Preface

As the twenty-first century rolls on, media reports about melting polar ice caps, rising ocean temperatures, and strange weather patterns seem commonplace. Politicians, celebrities, and representatives from various industries are all talking about how the world needs to reduce its energy use to prevent global warming or climate change. Many scientists and environmental groups say that the Earth's climate is warming because human activities are increasing the amount of carbon dioxide in the atmosphere. They believe that global warming will have disastrous effects for life on planet Earth. However, there are prominent skeptics who aren't convinced. They think the Earth's climate is changing due to natural cyclical events, rather than to human activity, and that the media is exaggerating the global warming threat.

According to the United Nations International Panel on Climate Change (IPCC), climate change or global warming intensifies the "greenhouse effect," a natural process that keeps the Earth's climate in an agreeable range for life. In the Earth's upper atmosphere, tiny amounts of water vapor, carbon dioxide, methane, and other gases continually absorb heat and reflect it back to the planet's surface. These "greenhouse gases" act like a blanket and keep the Earth's temperatures relatively warm and hospitable to life.

Since the beginning of the industrial age human activities have increased the levels of some of the greenhouse gases in the atmosphere. In particular, the level of carbon dioxide in the upper atmosphere has increased due to the combustion of fossil fuels. Whenever energy is extracted from coal, oil, or natural gas to generate electricity, provide fuel for transportation, or to drive manufacturing processes, carbon dioxide is emitted. Much of this carbon dioxide ends up in the upper atmosphere. Deforestation is another reason for carbon dioxide increases in the upper atmosphere. Plants carry out photosynthesis using carbon dioxide and sunlight. Trees remove a significant amount of carbon dioxide from the atmosphere during photosynthesis. As more and more trees are cut down, particularly in tropical regions of the world, less carbon dioxide is removed and more ends up in the upper atmosphere.

According to the IPCC, the increased levels of carbon dioxide in the atmosphere are causing the Earth to warm because more heat is being reflected back to the Earth. They call this an "enhanced greenhouse effect," and they believe it is caused by human activities, such as energy production and deforestation. The U.S. Environmental Protection Agency (EPA) says that a warmer Earth may lead to changes in rainfall patterns, a rise in sea levels, and a wide range of impacts on plants, wildlife, and humans. According to data from the National Oceanic and Atmospheric Administration (NOAA) and the National Aeronautics and Space Administration (NASA), the Earth's average surface temperature has increased by about 1.2 to 1.4°F in the past 100 years. Two of the warmest years since 1850 were 1998 and 2005.

Former Vice President Al Gore has received international acclaim (receiving the Nobel Peace Prize in 2007) for raising awareness of climate change. He believes that global warming will have significant impacts on the planet and on humankind. For instance, Gore believes a hotter planet will more than likely lead to a proliferation of mosquitoes, which in turn will lead to more deaths from malaria and other heat-related diseases.

Many environmental groups, such as the Natural Resources Defense Council (NRDC) and the Sierra Club, are particularly concerned about the impacts global warming is having in the Arctic region. According to the NRDC, average temperatures in the Arctic are rising twice as fast as they are elsewhere in the world, and Arctic ice is getting thinner. The melting of once-permanent ice sheets affects native people, wildlife, and plants. Polar bears live only in the Arctic and depend on the sea ice for all of their needs. The rapid warming of the Arctic and melting of sea ice pose an overwhelming threat to the polar bear, which could become the first mammal to lose 100 percent of its habitat to global warming, says the NRDC. In 2007 and 2008, media reports about threatened polar bears were common.

Global warming skeptics say the media's reporting on polar bears is an example of alarmist hype and pandering to environmentalists. Outspoken global warming skeptic, U.S. Senator from Oklahoma James Inhofe, says the polar bears are not in peril. In fact, he says, their numbers are increasing. Inhofe cites U.S. Fish and Wildlife Service estimates that show the polar bear population at about 20,000 to 25,000 bears—up from the estimated 5,000 to 10,000 polar bears in the 1950s and 1960s.

Inhofe and other global warming skeptics, such as author Michael Crichton, say that global warming is a myth. They say that the Earth's climate is a complex and chaotic system. It is foolish to think that humans could have any impact on it and it is inaccurate to think that a change in a single variable, i.e., atmospheric levels of carbon dioxide, would cause the Earth to react in any predictable way. Philosopher Martin Cohen argues that there are so many unknown factors in climate— from the behavior of algae in the sea to the effects of sunspot activity—that supposed climate models cannot accurately predict the result of increased carbon dioxide levels.

National news reporter John Stossel has claimed that alarm over the prospect of global warming is not warranted by the science. Global warming is happening and we are responsible for at least some of it, says Stossel. Yet this does not mean that global warming will cause enough damage to the Earth and humanity to require drastic cuts in energy use. Stossel believes that if the world is warming, humans will adjust to it. "If sea levels rise, we can build dikes and move back from the coasts.

It worked for Holland. Farmers can plant different crops or move north. Russian farmers farmed northern Siberia for centuries. When the area became cold and desolate, the farmers moved south. Far better to keep studying global warming, let the science develop, and adjust to it if it happens, rather than wreck life as we know it by trying to stop it," says Stossel.

Some scientists say there are benefits of global warming that aren't being reported. Harvard astrophysicist Sallie Baliunas believes that the extra carbon dioxide in the atmosphere may actually benefit the world because carbon dioxide helps plants to grow and warmer winters would give farmers a longer harvest season. Dr. Baliunas thinks the reason we don't hear so much about global warming benefits is because of money. Since 1990, says Baliunas, approximately $25 billion dollars has been spent researching the negative aspects of global warming.

The global warming debate is an important part of renewable energy discussions in the United States. Many people believe that renewable energy is beneficial and can mitigate the impacts of global warming and perhaps prevent it. However, others are skeptical about the benefits of renewable energy, and some people believe some forms of renewable energy are detrimental to the environment. The authors of the viewpoints in the following chapter provide their opinions on the benefits of renewable energy.

> "Each passing day brings yet more evi-
> dence that we are now facing a plan-
> etary emergency—a climate crisis that
> demands immediate action to sharply
> reduce carbon dioxide emissions world-
> wide in order to turn down the earth's
> thermostat and avert catastrophe."

Renewable Energy Is Necessary to Reduce Global Warming

Al Gore

In the following viewpoint, Al Gore contends that carbon dioxide-caused climate change threatens to destroy the habitability of earth and the United States must lead the charge to fight it. Gore says that some combination of wind- and solar-generated electricity and ethanol and biodiesel automobile fuels represent the best approach to fight climate change. Shifting to renewable energy can sharply reduce carbon dioxide emissions and help ease climate change, says Gore. Former vice president and winner of the Nobel Peace Prize, Al Gore has helped bring the issue of climate change to the world's attention.

Al Gore, "As Prepared Remarks by Former Vice President Al Gore, New York University School of Law, September 18, 2006." Reproduced by permission.

As you read, consider the following questions:

1. What is a "smart grid"?

2. What does Gore think we need to focus on, in addition to food, feed, and fiber, to revitalize the farm economy?

3. What companies does Gore identify as being leaders in reducing global warming pollution?

A few days ago [September 2006], scientists announced alarming new evidence of the rapid melting of the perennial ice of the north polar cap, continuing a trend of the past several years that now confronts us with the prospect that human activities, if unchecked in the next decade, could destroy one of the earth's principle mechanisms for cooling itself. Another group of scientists presented evidence that human activities are responsible for the dramatic warming of sea surface temperatures in the areas of the ocean where hurricanes form. A few weeks earlier, new information from yet another team showed dramatic increases in the burning of forests throughout the American West, a trend that has increased decade by decade, as warmer temperatures have dried out soils and vegetation. All these findings come at the end of a summer with record breaking temperatures and the hottest twelve month period ever measured in the U.S., with persistent drought in vast areas of our country. *Scientific American* introduces the lead article in its special issue this month [September 2006] with the following sentence: "The debate on global warming is over.". . .

Each passing day brings yet more evidence that we are now facing a planetary emergency—a climate crisis that demands immediate action to sharply reduce carbon dioxide emissions worldwide in order to turn down the earth's thermostat and avert catastrophe. . . .

U.S. Must Be Moral Leader

We in the United States of America have a particularly important responsibility, after all, because the world still regards us—in spite of our recent moral lapses—as the natural leader of the community of nations. Simply put, in order for the world to respond urgently to the climate crisis, the United States must lead the way. No other nation can. . . .

So, what would a responsible approach to the climate crisis look like if we had one in America?

Well, first of all, we should start by immediately freezing CO_2 [carbon dioxide] emissions and then beginning sharp reductions. Merely engaging in high-minded debates about theoretical future reductions while continuing to steadily increase emissions represents a self-delusional and reckless approach. . . .

A responsible approach to solutions would avoid the mistake of trying to find a single magic "silver bullet" and recognize that the answer will involve what [environmentalist] Bill McKibben has called "silver-buckshot"—numerous important solutions, all of which are hard, but no one of which is by itself the full answer for our problem. . . .

There are already some solutions that seem to stand out as particularly promising. . . .

Distributed, Dispersed Renewable Energy

Small windmills and photovoltaic solar cells distributed widely throughout the electricity grid would sharply reduce CO_2 emissions and at the same time increase our energy security. Likewise, widely dispersed ethanol and biodiesel production facilities would shift our transportation fuel stocks to renewable forms of energy while making us less dependent on and vulnerable to disruptions in the supply of expensive crude oil from the Persian Gulf, Venezuela and Nigeria, all of which are extremely unreliable sources upon which to base our future economic vitality. . . .

Renewables Offer Solution to Climate Change

Climate change is arguably one of the greatest environmental threats the world is facing. The impacts of disruptive change leading to catastrophic events such as storms, droughts, sea level rise and floods are already being felt across the world.

While the Kyoto Protocol, which aims to reduce greenhouse gas emissions, is slowly impacting on energy markets, scientists are increasingly advising policymakers that carbon emission reductions of beyond 60% are needed over the next 40–50 years. How will we achieve such a dramatic reduction in carbon emissions?

At the heart of the issue is an energy system based on fossil fuels, that is mainly responsible for greenhouse gas emissions.

On the contrary, renewable energy provides one of the leading solutions to the climate change issue. By providing "carbon-neutral" sources of power, heat, cooling and transport fuels, renewable energy options such as wind, solar, biomass, hydro, wave and tidal offer a safe transition to a low carbon economy.

European Renewable Energy Council,
"Renewable Energy: A Key Solution to Climate Change," 2004.
www.erec.org.

Just as a robust information economy was triggered by the introduction of the Internet, a dynamic new renewable energy economy can be stimulated by the development of an "electranet," or smart grid, that allows individual homeowners and business-owners anywhere in America to use their own renewable sources of energy to sell electricity into the grid when they have a surplus and purchase it from the grid when they don't. . . .

Greater Reliance on Renewable Fuels

Shifting to a greater reliance on ethanol, cellulosic ethanol, butanol, and green diesel fuels will not only reduce global warming pollution and enhance our national and economic security, it will also reverse the steady loss of jobs and income in rural America. Several important building blocks for America's role in solving the climate crisis can be found in new approaches to agriculture. As pointed out by the "25 by 25" movement (aimed at securing 25% of America's power and transportation fuels from agricultural sources by the year 2025) we can revitalize the farm economy by shifting its mission from a focus on food, feed and fiber to a focus on food, feed, fiber, fuel, and ecosystem services. . . .

Wind energy is already fully competitive as a mainstream source of electricity and will continue to grow in prominence and profitability.

Solar photovoltaic energy is—according to researchers—much closer than it has ever been to a cost competitive breakthrough, as new nanotechnologies are being applied to dramatically enhance the efficiency with which solar cells produce electricity from sunlight. . . .

Many of our leading businesses are already making dramatic changes to reduce their global warming pollution. General Electric, Dupont, Cinergy, Caterpillar, and Wal-Mart are among the many who are providing leadership for the business community in helping us devise a solution for this crisis. . . .

It's a Moral Issue

This is not a political issue. This is a moral issue. It affects the survival of human civilization. It is not a question of left vs. right; it is a question of right vs. wrong. Put simply, it is wrong to destroy the habitability of our planet and ruin the prospects of every generation that follows ours. . . .

This is an opportunity for bipartisanship and transcendence, an opportunity to find our better selves and in rising to meet this challenge, create a better brighter future—a future worthy of the generations who come after us and who have a right to be able to depend on us.

"Renewable energy and energy efficiency technologies are driving significant economic growth in the United States."

Renewable Energy Is Economically Beneficial

Roger Bezdek

In the following viewpoint, Roger Bezdek describes the results of a study he undertook for the American Solar Energy Society (ASES). Bezdek and the ASES believe that the United States government should invest in renewable energy and energy efficiency industries. According to Bezdek, by investing in these industries, the government can inject trillions of dollars into the U.S. economy and generate millions of new jobs by the year 2030. Roger Bezdek is a researcher for a consulting company. The ASES is a nonprofit organization with a mission to increase the use of solar and other renewable energies.

As you read, consider the following questions:

1. What are some of the measures Bezdek uses to show that renewable energy and energy efficiency technologies are a significant part of the United States economy?

Roger Bezdek, introduction and executive summary, *Renewable Energy and Energy Efficiency: Economic Drivers for the 21st Century*, Boulder, CO: Management Information Services, Inc. for the American Solar Energy Society, 2007. Copyright © 2007 American Solar Energy Society. Reproduced by permission.

2. According to Bezdek, how many new jobs were generated in 2006 in the renewable energy and energy efficiency industries?

3. What does Bezdek mean by the "moderate scenario"?

I t's all good news.

Renewable energy and energy efficiency technologies (RE&EE) are driving significant economic growth in the United States. In 2006, these industries generated 8.5 million new jobs, nearly $970 billion in revenue, more than $100 billion in industry profits, and more than $150 billion in increased federal, state, and local government tax revenues. Additionally, RE&EE provided important stimulus to the beleaguered U.S. manufacturing industry, displaced imported oil, and helped reduce the U.S. trade deficit.

To put this in perspective, RE&EE sales outpaced the combined sales of the three largest U.S. corporations. Total sales for Wal-Mart, Exxon-Mobil, and General Motors in 2006 were $905 billion.

Policy Can Push Renewable Energy and Energy Efficiency Growth

If U.S. policymakers aggressively commit to programs that support the sustained orderly development of RE&EE, the news gets even better. According to research conducted by the American Solar Energy Society (ASES) and Management Information Services, Inc. (MISI), the renewable energy and energy efficiency industry could—in a crash effort—generate up to $4.5 trillion in revenue in the United States and create 40 million new jobs by the year 2030. These 40 million jobs would represent nearly one out of every four jobs in 2030, and many would be jobs that could not easily be outsourced.

What will it take to get from here to there?

We will need to understand both the current status and structure of the RE&EE sectors and the public policies and regulatory programs most likely to support and encourage orderly growth in these sectors. The ASES/MISI research provides a working definition of the RE&EE industry, a baseline of comprehensive RE&EE data describing the size and scope of the RE&EE industry in 2006, and an analysis of three possible growth scenarios. . . .

Defining the Renewable Energy and Energy Efficiency Industry

The first objective, and one of the major contributions of our study, is to develop a rigorous definition of the RE&EE industry. We anticipate that the definition outlined here will become the standard for future economic analyses of the RE&EE industry.

Precisely what is the "renewable energy" or the "energy efficiency" industry? From windows and doors to airliners and automobiles to home appliances and industrial motors, manufacturers and marketers are quick to tout products' "renewable" or "energy efficiency" attributes. In addition, a growing number of organizations advertise their programs as contributing to energy efficiency or supporting renewable energy. As we worked toward a meaningful definition of the RE&EE industry, we had to sort through these claims and decide which products and programs deserved to be included in our definition.

It is an easy call if the RE&EE product or service exists as a distinct, specified entity, but this was rarely the case. Typically, only some of a company's or organization's offerings could be classified as part of the RE&EE industry, and quantifying the size of the RE&EE contribution was a challenge.

In the end, there is no single definitive answer to these questions. . . .We decided that these issues could perhaps be illustrated by focusing on RE&EE jobs. For example, under the broad industry definition, an employee working in a private

RE company or for an RE&EE advocacy organization would constitute a RE&EE job, as would an employee of the federal or a state RE&EE agency.

Of course, there were ambiguities here too. Most people would agree that the positions in a firm that assembles and installs solar thermal collectors would be considered RE&EE jobs. But what about the jobs involved in producing those solar panels, especially if the factory involved uses coal-based energy, one of the most controversial fossil fuels in terms of emissions?

In addition, we found that the vast majority of the jobs created by RE&EE are standard jobs for accountants, engineers, computer analysts, clerks, factory workers, truck drivers, mechanics, etc. Thus, in our definition, the RE&EE industry encompasses all aspects of renewable energy and energy efficiency, and includes both the direct and indirect jobs created in both these sectors.

Estimating the Size of the RE&EE Industry

Once we had a definition of the RE&EE industry, we turned our attention to estimating the size and composition of the RE&EE industry [in 2006]. To do this, we first addressed the RE and EE industries separately, and then combined them.

In our study, we define renewable energy technologies primarily as hydroelectricity, biomass, geothermal, wind, photovoltaics, and solar thermal. Except for hydro and industry biomass, the RE U.S. energy contribution is small, although it is growing rapidly.

RE gross revenues totaled nearly $40 billion in 2006, and the RE industry was responsible for more than 450,000 direct and indirect jobs. The jobs created were disproportionately for scientific, technical, professional, and skilled workers, and more than 90 percent of the jobs were in private industry.

Estimating the size of the EE industry is much more difficult than estimating the size of the RE industry. The RE in-

Renewable Energy Solves Problems and Has Economic Benefits

America's current reliance on coal, oil, gas, and nuclear power for electricity generation has left the country with a legacy of environmental and public health problems. This legacy also includes volatile price fluctuations, costing consumers dearly on electricity bills. We can help solve these problems by reducing demand through energy efficiency and diversifying our electricity mix with renewable energy sources. Fortunately, investing in clean energy policies also would generate new high-paying jobs, save consumers and businesses billions of dollars, and boost America's economy while reducing power plant pollution.

U.S. PIRG Education Fund, "Redirecting America's Energy:
The Economic and Consumer Benefits of Clean Energy Policies,"
February 2005.

dustry is fairly well defined and consists of distinct sectors, but the EE "industry" is much more nebulous and difficult to define. Most EE spending is included in partial segments of large industries, such as vehicles, buildings, lighting, appliances, etc. . . .

The results of our research are impressive. In 2006 the combined RE&EE industry generated nearly a trillion dollars in industry sales, 8.5 million new jobs, more than $100 billion in industry profits, and more than $150 billion in increased federal, state, and local government tax revenues. In addition, RE&EE reduce the risks associated with fuel price volatility and can facilitate an industrial boom, create millions of jobs, foster new technology, revitalize the manufacturing sector, enhance economic growth, and help reduce the trade and budget deficits.

> "Renewable energy costs two to three
> times as much as energy from gas- and
> coal-fired power plants."

Renewable Energy Is Economically Costly

Independence Institute

In the following viewpoint, the Independence Institute argues that the government shouldn't invest in renewable energy industries. Renewable energy has environmental impacts and is economically costly. Instead, the Independence Institute believes that solar, wind, and other renewable energy technologies should compete on their own without government assistance. The Independence Institute is a nonprofit public policy organization that seeks alternatives to government interventions.

As you read, consider the following questions:

1. According to the Independence Institute, how do wind farms compare with gas-fired power plants in terms of land use?

2. What are some of the reasons wind power is so expensive, according to the Independence Institute?

Independence Institute, "The False Panacea of Renewable Energy," Center for the American Dream of Mobility and Home Ownership Issue Backgrounder 2004-B. www.i2i.org. Copyright © 2004 Independence Institute. All rights reserved. Reproduced by permission.

3. What major scandal was the result of government renewable-energy incentives, according to the Independence Institute?

Renewable energy sources such as wind, hydro, solar, and biomass are viewed by many as superior to coal, gas, and other non-renewables. Eventually, some or all of these forms of energy may be viable. However, government subsidies and incentives for renewables can create more problems than they solve.

The Environmental Cost of Renewables

Most renewable sources of energy come at a steep environmental cost. Kilowatt for kilowatt, wind farms consume up to 200 times as much land as gas-fired power plants. Wind turbines also kill thousands of birds each year, especially raptors such as eagles, hawks, and vultures. Based on estimates of the number of birds killed by existing wind farms, energy expert Robert Bradley calculates that, if one-quarter of U.S. energy came from wind, the turbines would kill more than a million birds a year. Efforts by the wind power industry to solve this problem have so far proven unsuccessful.

Where wind turbines kill birds, hydroturbines kill fish. In an effort to recover Pacific Northwest salmon, the Bonneville Power Administration has an expensive program of capturing and trucking fish around its Columbia River dams. The pools created behind hydroelectric dams are also harmful to the habitats of many fish. Because of the cost to fisheries, many environmentalists support "non-hydro renewables."

Biomass energy [a variety of energy technologies involving plant and animal waste] produces significant air pollution, including carbon dioxide, nitrogen oxides, and particulates. In some cases, biomass can produce more carbon dioxide, a greenhouse gas, than coal-fired power plants.

Like wind, solar power requires a lot of land—some 5 to 10 acres per megawatt [1,000 kilowatts] of power. Solar energy panel manufacture also produces serious toxic wastes, including arsenic, gallium, and cadmium.

The Economic Cost of Renewables

Renewable energy costs two to three times as much as energy from gas- and coal-fired power plants. According to energy researcher Robert Bradley:

- When the cost of subsidies are included, wind power costs twice as much, per kilowatt hour, as building new gas-fired power plants;

- Biomass energy also costs twice as much as gas-fired power;

- Solar power costs three times as much as new gas-fired power plants;

- Building new hydroelectric plants costs three to six times as much as new gas-fired plants.

One of the reasons why wind power is so expensive is that it is so unreliable. Bradley cites research indicating that wind turbines produce only 15 to 25 percent of their capacity, so other sources of energy must be available to back them up.

The costs of renewable energy have been declining, but so have the costs of more traditional sources of energy. According to the Department of Energy, the cost of generating electricity from gas- and coal-plants fell by more than 50 percent between 1981 and 1997.

The Cost of Government Interference

The market does an excellent job of dealing with shortages and disappearing non-renewable resources. As resources decline, their price increases, which leads people to find and improve alternatives.

A good example of this is the transition in the telecommunications industry from copper to fiber optics: A few de-

Ordinary Citizens Pay Hidden Costs of Renewable Wind Energy

As more wind turbines are proposed in the U.S. and other countries, ordinary citizens have learned that "wind farms" are not environmentally benign. Instead, wind energy has high economic, environmental, ecological, scenic and property value costs. Wind turbines produce only small amounts of electricity and that electricity is unreliable and low in value.

Quite likely, many members of Congress, state legislators, governors, regulators and local officials don't yet realize that they have been misled about the true benefits and costs of wind energy—or the extent of their combined generosity to the wind industry.

In the U.S., "wind farms" are now being built primarily for tax avoidance purposes, not because of their environmental, energy or economic benefits. The tax breaks and subsidies have more value to "wind farm" owners than the revenue from the sale of electricity they produce.

These generous tax breaks and subsidies are at the expense of ordinary taxpayers and electric customers and are hidden in their tax bills and monthly electric bills. Government officials seem unaware or uncaring about either the large transfer of wealth to "wind farm" owners from ordinary citizens—or the fact that large amounts of capital are being spent on projects that produce only small amounts of unreliable, low value electricity.

Glenn R. Schleede, "'Big Money'
Discovers the Huge Tax Breaks and Subsidies for 'Wind Energy'
While Taxpayers and Electric Customers Pick Up the Tab,"
Minnesotans For Sustainability, April 15, 2005.
www.mnforsustain.org.

cades ago, experts worried that a shortage of copper would threaten the industry. Today [2004] copper mines are shut down for lack of demand.

Government interference in this process can do more harm than good. Incentives to use renewable resources, for example, contributed to the Enron scandal [a notorious bankruptcy case of 2002]. Federal laws encouraged production of wind power by requiring electric utilities to pay more for wind power that is generated by non-utilities than for other sources of power.

To take advantage of this, Enron purchased a wind farm in California. Soon after, however, Enron bought an electric utility in Portland, making it ineligible for the price premium. So it pretended to sell the wind farm, while in fact it kept an "illegal and secret interest" in the farm, says the U.S. Justice Department. . . .

Government support for certain technologies can also stifle the innovation those technologies need to become truly competitive. Renewables cost more than non-renewables, but technological improvements should bring costs down. Government support shields producers from competition and thus discourages innovation. Ironically, the very supports that are intended to promote renewable energy may be inhibiting it.

Government subsidies may lead to another problem: a locking-in of inefficient technologies when other technologies may make more sense. Technology lock in takes place when one technology becomes so dominant that a superior technology cannot replace it. . . .No one knows today whether wind, solar, tidal, or something entirely unexpected will eventually replace fossil fuels. By favoring some technologies over others, government may unwittingly promote the locking in of an inferior technology. The best solution for renewable energy and energy consumers is to let market forces work.

> "Renewable energy, also called 'green energy,' or 'clean energy,' does not deplete natural resources and creates little to no pollution when it is generated."

Renewable Energy Is Beneficial for the Environment

Science Clarified

In the following viewpoint, Science Clarified *discusses the benefits of renewable energy and claims that the use of fossil fuels (coal, oil, and natural gas) for energy production is harmful to the environment and depletes natural resources. According to* Science Clarified, *humans must seek environmentally friendly alternatives to fossil fuels, and limitless and virtually pollution-free renewable energy offers the best hope for our future energy needs.* Science Clarified *is an online encyclopedia.*

As you read, consider the following questions:

1. According to *Science Clarified*, what percentage of the world's nitrous oxide emissions come from burning fossil fuels?

2. According to *Science Clarified*, how many barrels of oil were consumed in the year 2000?

3. What are the key benefits of renewable energy when compared to burning fossil fuels, according to *Science Clarified*?

Weighing the benefits and drawbacks of one power source versus another is a complicated process. There are many factors to consider, including everything from understanding the environmental effects of a particular type of power production and consumption, to addressing the power needs of the people and finding methods for delivering the power. Throughout this process, decision makers rely upon scientists to supply the necessary data to make informed decisions. What forms the basis of this science includes the knowledge that carbon dioxide, which is released into the atmosphere when fossil fuels are burned, is creating a lot of harm to the planet and its systems.

Burning Fossil Fuels Emits Harmful Gases

Gases that form the atmosphere completely surround the planet. A part of the atmosphere called the ozone layer acts as a sort of shield from the sun, filtering out harmful radiations. Today, human activities release about 433,000 metric tons of nitrous oxide into the atmosphere each year. Nearly 40 percent of the world's nitrous oxide emissions come from burning fossil fuels. The atmosphere has a certain amount of nitrous oxide naturally, but too much nitrous oxide causes a depletion of the ozone layer. Over the last decade scientists have reported that the hole in the ozone layer is growing rapidly.

Carbon dioxide is another harmful gas released into the atmosphere. It comes back to the surface as acid rain, poisoning water supplies, killing plants and animals, and eroding and blackening buildings. In addition, carbon dioxide reflects light and heat back to the planet's surface. As the carbon dioxide levels increase in the atmosphere, more heat from the sun is held in, changing the climate of the entire planet by making it warmer. This is called the greenhouse effect and is considered a form of pollution. [Naturalist] Laughton Johnston claims that, "Carbon dioxide levels in the atmosphere are at their highest in 20 million years."

The planet Earth operates on delicate systems of natural balance. Scientists believe warming the atmosphere by even a few degrees could cause enormous changes to the environment. Some scientists also believe an increase in the temperature of the planet, brought on by the greenhouse effect, will lead to more weather-related natural disasters such as tornadoes, floods, droughts, and hurricanes. Scientists also predict a significant rise in sea level, which will reduce land size. Considering that half of the human population lives near a coastline, the effects could be dramatic. In the future, many nations may need to struggle with the question of where all of their people should live if their towns and cities become submerged under oceanic water.

For example, according to a report released by the British Broadcasting Corporation in 2003, the Arctic ice cover is shrinking by an area the size of the Netherlands every year. The Arctic ice cap has thinned from an average thickness of more than nine feet to less than six feet in. . .thirty years. In 2002, for the first time in recorded history, a twelve-thousand-year-old ice shelf the size of Luxembourg came adrift from the Antarctic and melted into pieces in just thirty-five days. The glaciers of Kilimanjaro, a mountain in Africa, and of the tropical Andes mountains in South America are melting so fast that experts believe they could disappear within. . .twenty years. In October 2001 about eleven thousand people in Tuvalu, a group of nine islands in the Pacific Ocean, tried to abandon their homes because of the rising ocean. The Australian government refused to let them into Australia and so most of the people have remained on the islands, living in fear of being submerged in the ocean.

Burning fossil fuels for energy releases much of the harmful gases that exist today. Scientists estimate that about 35 percent of the greenhouse gases, such as carbon dioxide, being released into the atmosphere are from the United States. With only about 5 percent of the world's population, the United States consumes about one quarter of the world's energy production. At this rate, according to [space engineer] Ralph Nansen, "we will destroy both the breathable air and the energy reserves of our only home." In fact, according to a recent BBC Radio Scotland report on global climate change, if the rest of the world consumed energy at the same rate as the United States, "we would need at least two more planet earth's to sustain us all."

Fossil Fuel Supplies Depleted

Not only are these high levels of consumption causing equally high levels of pollution, but the world's fossil fuel supplies are quickly being used up. For example, [the] total oil supply is estimated at between 2,000 and 2,800 billion barrels. About 900 billion barrels of oil have already been consumed, 28 million barrels of that just in the year 2000. Addressing resource depletion is not an easy task. As Tom Hansen, vice president of Tucson Electric Power, says, "It is like trying to change the wings of an airplane while you are in flight." He describes a difficult process, but one with what he considers a great payoff. "We have to wean ourselves off traditional fuels, because it is going to get harder for us to build more power plants and install more transmission lines."

The future of energy production will certainly determine what the overall health of the planet will be. Most scientists agree that the choices that support fossil fuel use will only worsen the environmental damage that has already occurred. Instead, choosing to look to renewable energy sources and energy conservation techniques offers the potential to improve the health of the planet. This belief concerning the future of

Environmental Benefits of Renewable Energy

Power plant air emissions are responsible for approximately one-third of nitrogen oxide emissions, two-thirds of sulfur dioxide emissions, and one-third of carbon dioxide emissions nationally. Renewables can avoid or reduce these air emissions, as well as reduce water consumption, thermal pollution, waste, noise, and adverse land-use impacts.

Moreover, renewables are sustainable energy resources: they avoid depletion of natural resources for future generations.

Union of Concerned Scientists, "Environmental Benefits of Renewable Energy," August 10, 2005. www.ucsusa.org.

renewable energy is voiced by author Melvin A. Benarde in his book, *Our Precarious Habitat.* "There are no instant cures, no ready-made solutions," Benarde writes. "This does not mean there is no hope for a future. On the contrary, there is a great deal; but it will take time and money—lots of money—and a willingness on the part of the people to see it through."

Renewable Energy Does Not Run Out

Because energy is usable power, the form that the energy is in can be used up. When a combustion engine car runs out of gasoline, it loses its power and can no longer operate until more fuel is put into the system. If a power plant that generates electricity by burning coal runs out of coal, then it can no longer generate electricity until more coal is put into the power plant burners.

Renewable energy, on the other hand, is energy that is replaced at the same rate that it is used. Renewable energy is replaced through natural processes or through sound management practices, and so it is a source of power that does not run out. A perfect example of renewable energy is energy from the sun, which comes in an abundant supply every day.

Other examples of renewable sources of energy include the wind, the waves and tides, the gravitational pull of the earth, the heat at the earth's core (geothermal energy), landfill gases, and, to a limited degree, trees and plant material. Many of these renewable sources of energy can be used in their raw form. They are natural forces that create energy without the help of humans. All that is needed is for someone to decide how that energy can be used. Building a sail for a boat makes use of the wind. Building a waterwheel on a river makes use of the flowing water that is pulled downhill by the earth's gravity. Building a house out of glass—a greenhouse—traps the heat from sunlight inside, providing warmth and allowing plants to grow where they might not otherwise grow.

Renewable Energy Creates Little or No Pollution

Renewable energy, also called "green energy," or "clean energy," does not deplete natural resources and creates little to no pollution when it is generated. Throughout history, renewable sources of energy have been used by various peoples to supply power for their specific needs, but always on a small scale. The unique challenge of today is finding a way to supply renewable energy to entire populations. Large-scale energy production requires specialized equipment such as energy storage and transmission facilities. The technology for generating the power must also be efficient and cost-effective to produce and operate.

In the face of big-oil-company interests and the politics of government, it has taken a long time for renewable energy options to even be considered on a large scale. The scientific and technological development of solar power, for example, looked promising when in 1977 President Jimmy Carter initiated a plan to develop solar energy and other alternative fuels. His goal for the nation was to have 20 percent of its power coming from solar power generation by the year 2000, and he started by putting solar panels on the White House. By the late 1970s, however, big oil companies had bought up most of the patents for the solar technologies being developed. The Reagan administration took the solar panels off of the White House and spent billions of dollars on the military, foreign aid, and for research and production of atomic weapons instead of on renewable energy.

Since that time, government support for the research and development of renewable energy has not been easy to get, and the technology has been slow to come into its own. Despite these setbacks, independent companies are now making renewable energy products that, while still costly to purchase, offer cheap, clean, renewable energy to the consumer. In his book *Charging Ahead*, writer, teacher, and environmental science and policy consultant John J. Berger says of renewable energy sources that "modern science and engineering technology have of late made them much more efficient, convenient, and economical." Steve Kretzmann, coordinator for the Greenpeace Global Warming Campaign, shares a similar point of view: "One of the greatest myths surrounding clean energy is that it is not ready to do the job. Renewables *are* ready—the technical barriers are almost entirely removed. The true barriers to energy reform are now, and always have been, political."

Many experts agree that renewable energy would provide numerous benefits. Berger, for example, says that:

> Because renewables do not use fossil fuels (most are entirely fuel-free) they are largely immune to the threat of future oil or gas shortages and fossil fuel price hikes. For the same reason, because most renewable technologies require no combustion, they are far kinder to the environment than coal, oil, and natural gas. Smog and acid rain could be eliminated with renewables. The collective lungs of America could breathe a sigh of relief.

In addition to being virtually nonpolluting, renewable energy is thought to be cheaper for producers and consumers. As reported in a book commissioned in 1992 by the United Nations Solar Energy Group on Environment and Development, "Given adequate support, renewable energy technologies can meet much of the growing demand at prices lower than those usually forecast for conventional energy." As the human population continues to increase and the energy needs of the world climb, renewable energy is seen more and more as the only alternative.

> *"Let's stop sanctifying the false and mi-*
> *nor gods and heretically chant 'Renew-*
> *ables are not Green.'"*

Renewable Energy Is Not Beneficial for the Environment

Jesse H. Ausubel

In the following viewpoint, Jesse H. Ausubel argues that, contrary to what many people think, renewables are not green—sustainable and good for the environment. Ausubel says that in order for renewables to contribute meaningfully to energy production, they would use up vast amounts of land and cause serious environmental damage. Ausubel believes that nuclear power is the greenest energy choice because it can generate large amounts of power while using a relatively small amount of land. Ausubel contends that society's energy system needs to shrink in size and cost rather than grow larger under renewables. Jesse H. Ausubel is director of the Program for the Human Environment and a senior research associate at Rockefeller University in New York City.

Jesse H. Ausubel, "Renewable and Nuclear Heresies," *International Journal of Nuclear Governance, Economy and Ecology*, vol. 1, no. 3, 2007, pp. 229–235. Copyright © 2007 Inderscience Enterprises Limited. All rights reserved. Reproduced by permission.

As you read, consider the following questions:

1. Does the author claim that a high carbon-to-hydrogen ratio is desirable or undesirable in a fuel?

2. According to the author, what kind of source is the largest provider of renewable energy in the United States and Canada?

3. According to the author, how much space would be needed if wind farms were to meet the current electricity demand in the United States?

Heretics maintain opinions at variance with those generally received. Putting heretics to death, hereticide, is common through history. In 1531 the Swiss Protestant heretic Huldreich Zwingli soldiering anonymously in battle against the Catholic cantons was speared in the thigh and then clubbed on the head. Mortally wounded, he was offered the services of a priest. His declination caused him to be recognised, whereupon he was killed and quartered, and his body parts mixed with dung and ceremonially burned. Recall that the first heresy against the Roman Church in Switzerland in 1522 was the eating of sausages during Lent, and the signal heresy was opposition to the baptism of children. As nuclear experts know deeply, humans are not rational in their beliefs, actions or reactions.

I will offer both renewable and nuclear heresies. I trust readers will not commit hereticide. Because culture defines heresies, readers coming from a nuclear tribe will probably applaud my renewable heresies and grumble about the nuclear. While my heresies may not rival favoring polygamy or sharing all worldly goods, they will disturb many. My main heresies are that renewable sources of energy are not green and that the nuclear industry should make a product besides electricity.

Decarbonisation: Decreasing the Carbon-to-Hydrogen Ratio

The dogma that gives me conviction to uphold heresies is decarbonisation, which I accept as the central measure of energy evolution. Consider our hydrocarbon fuels as blends of carbon and hydrogen, both of which burn to release energy. Molecules of the main so-called fossil fuels, coal, oil and natural gas, each have a typical ratio of carbon to hydrogen atoms. Methane, CH_4, is obviously 1 to 4. An oil such as kerosene is 1 to 2. A typical coal's ratio of C:H is about 2 to 1. Importantly, coal's precursor, wood, has an even more primitive C:H ratio, 10 to 1, once the moisture is removed. Carbon blackens miners' lungs, endangers urban air and threatens climate change. Hydrogen is as innocent as an element can be, ending combustion as water.

Suppose we placed all the hydrocarbon fuels humanity used each year since about 1800, when British colliers first mined thousands of tons of coal, in a blender, mixed them, and plotted the yearly ratio of carbon to hydrogen. While the trend may waver for a decade or two, over the long term H gains in the mix at the expense of C, like cars replacing horses, colour TV substituting for black-and-white, or email gaining the market over hard copies sent through the post office. The consequent decarbonisation is the single most important fact from 30 years of energy studies.

When my colleagues Cesare Marchetti, Nebojsa Nakicenovic, Arnulf Grubler and I discovered decarbonisation in the 1980s, we were pleasantly surprised. When we first spoke of decarbonisation, few believed and many ridiculed the word. Everyone "knew" the opposite to be true. Now prime ministers and presidents speak of decarbonisation. Neither Queen Victoria nor Abraham Lincoln decreed a policy of decarbonisation. Yet, the energy system pursued it. Human societies pursued decarbonisation for 170+ years before anyone noticed. . . .

Returning to carbon, if world economic production or all energy rather than all hydrocarbons form the denominator, the world is also decarbonising, that is, using less carbon per dollar of output or kilowatt. Moreover, China and India as well as France and Japan decarbonise. The slopes are quite similar, though China and India lag by several decades, as they do in the diffusion of other technologies besides energy. Economically and technically, carbon seems fated to fade gradually over this century. By 2100 we will feel nostalgia for carbon as some do now for steam locomotives. Londoners have mythologised their great fogs, induced by coal as late as the 1950s, and Berliners already reminisce about the "East Smell" of burnt lignite [low-grade coal] whose use collapsed after the fall of [the Berlin] Wall in 1989.

The explanation for the persistence of decarbonisation is simple and profound. The overall evolution of the energy system is driven by the increasing spatial density of energy consumption at the level of the end user, that is, the energy consumed per square metre, for example, in a city. Finally, fuels must conform to what the end user will accept, and constraints become more stringent as spatial density of consumption rises. Rich, dense cities accept happily only electricity and gases, now methane and later hydrogen. These fuels reach consumers easily through pervasive infrastructure grids, right to the burner tip in your kitchen.

My city, New York, by the way, already consumes in electricity alone on a July day about 15 watts per square metre averaged over its entire 820 square kilometres of land, including Central Park.

A few decades ago, some visionaries dreamed of an all-electric society. Today people convert about 35–40% of all primary fuel to electricity. The fraction will rise, but now even electricity enthusiasts (as I am) accept that finally not much more than half of all energy is likely to be electrified. Reasons include the impracticality of a generating system geared entirely to the instant consumption of energy and lack of amenability of many vehicles to reliance on electricity. . . .

Ultimately the behaviour of end-users drives the system. Happily, the system can thus be rational even when individuals are not. When end-users want electricity and hydrogen, over time the primary energy sources that can produce on the needed scale while meeting the ever more stringent constraints that attend growth in turn will win. Economies of scale are a juggernaut [overwhelming force] over the long run. Think, for better or worse, of Wal-Mart stores.

Appropriately, the historical growth of world primary energy consumption over the past 150 years shows rises in long waves of 50–60 years, each time formed around the development of a more desirable source of energy that scaled up [accommodated growth] readily. Coal lifted the first wave, and oil the second. A new growth wave is underway, lifted by methane, now almost everyone's favourite fuel. . . .

According to the historical trend in decarbonisation, large-scale production of carbon-free hydrogen should begin about the year 2020. So how will humanity keep lifting electricity production while also introducing more H_2 [hydrogen] into the system to lift the average above the norm of methane? The obvious competitors are nuclear and the so-called renewables, the false and minor, yet popular, idols.

Hydro Is Not Green

Let's consider the renewable idols: hydro, biomass, wind and solar. As a Green, I care intensely about land-sparing, about leaving land for Nature. In fact, a Green credo is "No new structures." Or, in milder form, "New structures or infrastructures should fit within the footprint of the old structures or infrastructures." So, I will examine renewables primarily by their use of land.

In the USA and much of the rest of the world, including Canada, renewables mean dammed rivers. Almost 80% of so-called US renewable energy is hydro, and hydro generates about 60% of all Canada's electricity.

For the USA as a whole, the capacity of all existing hydropower plants is about 97,500 MWe [megawatts electricity] and their average production is about 37,500 MWe. The average power intensity—the watts divided by the land area of the USA—is 0.005 watts per square metre, that is, the approximate power that can be obtained from a huge tract of land that drains into a reservoir for a power station.

Imagine the entire province of Ontario [Canada], about 900,000 square km, collecting its entire 680,000 billion litres of rain, an average annual rainfall of about 0.8 m. Imagine collecting all that water, every drop, behind a dam of about 60 metres height. Doing so might inundate half the province, and thus win the support of the majority of Canadians, who resent the force of Ontario. This comprehensive "Ontario Hydro" would produce about 11,000 MW or about four fifths the output of Canada's 25 nuclear power stations, or about 0.012 watts per square metre or more than twice the USA average. In my "flood Ontario" scenario, a square kilometre would provide the electricity for about 12 Canadians.

This low density and the attending ecological and cultural headaches explain the trend in most of the world from dam building to dam removal. About 40% of Canada's immense total land area is effectively dammed for electrons already. The World Commission on Dams issued a report in November 2000 that essentially signalled the end of hydropower development globally. While the Chinese are constructing more dams, few foresee even ten thousand megawatts' further growth from hydropower.

Though electricity and hydrogen from hydro would decarbonise, the idol of hydro is itself dammed. Hydro is not green.

Liberal Opposition to Wind Power

Like many of the other towns targeted by the wind turbine industry, Andes [New York] is a rural community that over the years has lost its economic base. At one time the hills and valleys were home to many small dairy farms, but most of them are no longer in operation, and no industry, light or heavy, has taken their place. Now the area relies for its revenue on retirees and second home owners who are educated, relatively well off and tend to be teachers therapists, lawyers, artists and social workers. In short, liberals. They are all soldiers in Al Gore's army, into organic foods, hybrid cars, clean air, clean water, the whole bit.

They are also against wind power.

Their reasons are the ones always given by those who wake up to find the wind interests at their door. Even if large wind farms were in place throughout the country, the electricity produced would be a very small percentage of the electricity we use. Because the turbines are huge, 400 feet or more, installing them involves tearing up the ridges on which they are placed. Once in operation, they cast shadows and produce noise. Their blades cause a "flicker" effect, kill birds and interfere with migration. The outsized towers ruin scenic views and depress real-estate values.

Stanley Fish, "Blowin' in the Wind," Think Again,
August 26, 2007. http://fish.blogs.nytimes.com.

Biomass Is Not Green

In the USA, after hydro's 80% comes biomass's 17% of renewables. Surprisingly, most of this biomass comes, not from backyard woodsmen or community paper drives, but from liquors in pulp mills burned to economise their own heat and power. In terms of decarbonisation, biomass of course retrogresses, with 10 Cs or more per H.

If one argues that biomass is carbon-neutral because photosynthesis in plants recycles the carbon, one must consider its other attributes, beginning with productivity of photosynthesis. Although farmers usually express this productivity in tons per hectare [a hectare is approximately 2.5 acres], in the energy industry the heat content of the trees, corn and hay instead quantify the energy productivity of the land. For example, the abundant and untended New England or New Brunswick forests produce firewood at the renewable rate of about 1200 watts (thermal) per hectare averaged around the year. The 0.12 watts per square metre of biomass is about ten times more powerful than rain, and excellent management can multiply the figure again ten times.

Imagine, as energy analyst Howard Hayden has suggested, farmers use ample water, fertiliser, and pesticides to achieve 12,000 watts *thermal* per hectare (10,000 square metres). Imagine replacing a 1000 MWe nuclear power plant with a 90% capacity factor. During a year, the nuclear plant will produce about 7.9 billion kWh [kilowatt hours of electricity]. To obtain the same electricity from a power plant that burns biomass at 30% heat-to-electricity efficiency, farmers would need about 250,000 hectares or 2500 square kilometres of land with very high productivity. Harvesting and collecting the biomass are not 100% efficient; some gets left in fields or otherwise lost.

Such losses mean that in round numbers a 1000 MWe nuclear plant equates to more than 2500 square kilometres of prime land. A typical Iowa county spans about 1000 square kilometres, so it would take at least two and a half counties to fire a station. A nuclear power plant consumes about ten hectares per unit or 40 hectares for a power park. Shifting entirely from baconburgers to kilowatts, Iowa's 55,000 square miles might yield 50,000 MWe. Prince Edward Island might produce about 2000 MWe.

The USA already consumes about ten and the world about 40 times the kilowatt hours that Iowa's biomass could generate. Prime land has better uses, like feeding the hungry. Ploughing marginal lands would require ten or 20 times the expanse and increase erosion. One hundred twenty square metres of New Brunswick or Manitoba might electrify one square metre of New York City.

Note also that pumping water and making fertiliser and pesticides also consume energy. If processors concentrate the corn or other biomass into alcohol or diesel, another step erodes efficiency. Ethanol production yields a tiny net of 0.05 watts per square metre.

As in hydro, in biomass the lack of economies of scale loom large. Because more biomass quickly hits the ceiling of watts per square metre, it can become more extensive but not cheaper. If not false, the idol of biomass is not sustainable on the scale needed and will not contribute to decarbonisation. Biomass may photosynthesise but it is not green.

Wind Is Not Green

Although, or because, wind provides only 0.2% of US electricity, the idol of wind evokes much worship. The basic fact of wind is that it provides about 1.2 watts per square metre or 12,000 watts per hectare of year-round average electric power. Consider, for example, the $212 million wind farm about 30 kilometres south of Lamar, CO, where 108 1.5 MWe wind turbines stand 80 metres tall, their blades sweeping to 115 metres. The wind farm spreads over 4800 hectares. At 30% capacity, peak power density is the typical 1.2 watts per square metre.

One problem is that two of the four wind speed regimes produce no power at all. Calm air means no power of course, and gales faster than 25 metres per second (about 90 kilometres per hour) mean shutting down lest the turbine blow apart. Perhaps three to ten times more compact than biomass, a wind farm occupying about 770 square kilometres could produce as much energy as one 1000 MWe nuclear plant. To meet 2005 US electricity demand of about four million MWhr [megawatts per hour] with around-the-clock-wind would have required wind farms covering over 780,000 square kilometres, about Texas plus Louisiana, or about 1.2 times the area of Alberta. Canada's demand is about 10% of the USA and corresponds to about the area of New Brunswick....

Rapidly exhausted economies of scale stop wind. One hundred windy square metres, a good size for a Manhattan apartment, can power a lamp or two, but not the clothes washer and dryer, microwave oven, plasma TVs or computers or dozens of other devices in the apartment, or the apartments above or below it. New York City would require every square metre of Connecticut to become a windfarm if the wind blew in Hartford as in Lamar. The idol of wind would decarbonise but will be minor.

Solar Is Not Green

Although negligible as a source of electric power today, photovoltaics [PVs] also earn a traditional bow. Sadly, PVs remain stuck at about 10% efficiency, with no breakthroughs in 30 years. Today performance reaches about 5–6 watts per square metre. But no economies of scale inhere in PV systems. A 1000 MWe PV plant would require about 150 square kilometres plus land for storage and retrieval. Present USA electric consumption would require 150,000 square kilometres or a square almost 400 kilometres on each side. The PV industry now makes about 600 metres by 600 metres per year. About 600,000 times this amount would be needed to replace the 1000 MWe nuclear plant, but only a few square kilometres have ever been manufactured in total.

Viewed another way, to produce with solar cells the amount of energy generated in one litre of the core of a nuclear reactor requires one hectare of solar cells. To compete at making the millions of megawatts for the baseload of the world energy market, the cost and complication of solar collectors still need to shrink by orders of magnitude while efficiency soars.

Extrapolating the progress (or lack) in recent decades does not carry the solar and renewable system to market victory. Electrical batteries, crucial to many applications, weigh almost zero in the global energy market. Similarly, solar and renewable energy may attain marvelous niches, but seem puny for providing the base power for 8–10 billion people later this century.

Renewables Cost the Environment

While I have denominated power with land so far, solar and renewables, despite their sacrosanct status, cost the environment in other ways as well. The appropriate description for PVs comes from the song of the Rolling Stones, "Paint It Black." Painting large areas with efficient, thus black, absorbers evokes dark 19th century visions of the land. I prefer colourful desert to a 150,000 km² area painted black. Some of the efficient PVs contain nasty elements, such as cadmium. Wind farms irritate with low-frequency noise and thumps, blight landscapes, interfere with TV reception, and chop birds and bats. At the Altamont windfarm in California, the mills kill 40–60 golden eagles per year. Dams kill rivers.

Moreover, solar and renewables in every form require large and complex machinery to produce many megawatts. Berkeley engineer Per Petersen reports that for an average MWe a typical wind-energy system operating with a 6.5 metres-per-second average wind speed requires construction inputs of 460 metric tons of steel and 870 cubic metres of concrete. For comparison, the construction of existing 1970-vintage US nuclear power plants required 40 metric tons of steel and 190 cubic metres of concrete per average megawatt of electricity generating capacity. Wind's infrastructure takes five to ten times the steel and concrete as that of nuclear. Bridging the cloudy and dark as well as calm and gusty weather takes storage batteries and their heavy metals. Without vastly improved storage, the windmills and PVs are supernumeraries [unnecessary] for the coal, methane and uranium plants that operate reliably round the clock day after day.

Since 1980 the US DOE [Department of Energy] alone has spent about $6 billion on solar, $2 billion on geothermal, $1 billion on wind and $3 billion on other renewables. The nonhydro renewable energy remains about 2% of US capacity, much of that the wood byproducts used to fuel the wood products industry. Cheerful self-delusion about new solar and renewables since 1970 has yet to produce a single quad of the more than 90 quadrillion Btu [British thermal units, an energy measure] of the total energy the US now yearly consumes. In the 21 years from 1979 to 2000 the percentage of US energy from renewables actually fell from 8.5 to 7.3%. Environmentally harmless increments of solar and renewable megawatts look puny in a 20 or 30 million megawatt world, and even in today's 10 million megawatt world. If we want to scale up, then hydro, biomass, wind, and solar all gobble land from Nature. Let's stop sanctifying false and minor gods and heretically chant "Renewables are not Green."

| "There is indeed hydrogen everywhere, but not in a form that can be used as a fuel."

Hydrogen Is Not a Practical Fuel Source

Ed Hiserodt

In the following viewpoint, Ed Hiserodt questions the merits of a "hydrogen economy." Hiserodt contends that the amount of energy needed to produce enough hydrogen fuel to sustain the economy would be immense, and that the procedure to convert hydrogen into fuel is inefficient and expensive. He also believes that the impetus for a "hydrogen economy," the claim that we're running out of oil and alleged global warming, is exaggerated. Ed Hiserodt, an aerospace engineer, has been the president of Controls & Power, Inc., since 1983.

As you read, consider the following questions:

1. According to the author, how much would hydrogen fuel cost per gallon (not including shipping and handling costs)?

2. What are the author's arguments against using wind or solar power to produce hydrogen?

Ed Hiserodt, "The 'Hydrogen Economy,'" *The New American*, August 20, 2007. http:// thenewamerican.com. Copyright © 2007 American Opinion Publishing Incorporated. Reproduced by permission.

3. Why does the author believe that the role of carbon dioxide in climate change has been "grossly misrepresented?"

The "hydrogen economy" is a Green dream. Environmentalists looking for a source of energy to replace fossil fuels and nuclear energy rightly note that over 99.9 percent of the visible matter in the universe is hydrogen and that our oceans have an inexhaustible supply of hydrogen atoms. Moreover, they point out, hydrogen burns, and when it is burned in internal combustion engines or combined with oxygen in fuel cells, the only byproduct is water.

All that is true and wonderful and makes it seem as if hydrogen is the solution to the world's power needs. However, it ignores an important factor that diminishes the role hydrogen could otherwise play in solving our energy woes. Conveniently ignored in far too many cases is a problem similar to that besetting the ancient mariner in [Samuel Taylor] Coleridge's poem ["The Rime of the Ancient Mariner"]: there is indeed hydrogen everywhere, but not in a form that can be used as a fuel.

Problems with Hydrogen

Unlike petroleum, natural gas, and even helium, there are no hydrogen deposits that can be drilled and tapped for energy-production purposes. Because hydrogen readily combines with other molecules, to get usable hydrogen for energy-production purposes, we always have to separate it from its already chosen dance partner. A common process to commercially produce hydrogen is to use very high temperature steam to react with coke (almost pure carbon) to form hydrogen and carbon monoxide to produce what is known as "syngas."

A second commercially viable method of hydrogen production begins with natural gas, which is usually about 75 percent methane—a molecule with one carbon and four hydrogen atoms. The process to release those hydrogen atoms is also completed with high-temperature steam, as in the case of coke conversion. Ironically, after using large amounts of energy to free the hydrogen, the resultant hydrogen has a much lower energy content than the natural gas it was freed from. . . .

And there is another problem. Being the lightest substance in the universe, hydrogen must undergo compression or liquefaction before the product becomes useful as a fuel. Producing liquid hydrogen requires a further 25 percent energy input into the hydrogen-production process.

For now let us estimate the energy cost of compressed hydrogen as requiring 60 kWh per kilogram. The equivalent of a gallon of gas (in terms of hydrogen) would require an energy cost of about 55 kWh of electrical power to produce. With the industrial cost of electricity in the range of six cents per kWh, then compressed hydrogen would cost in the neighborhood of $3.30 per gallon of gasoline. And this is the cost without any of the possible prodigious shipping and handling costs generated by transporting the hydrogen to a fuel station near you.

The amount of energy needed to produce enough hydrogen fuel to sustain the economy would be immense. One normal-sized nuclear power plant, capable of producing 24,000 megawatt-hours of power per day, could produce about 450,000 gallon-equivalents of hydrogen per day. This would serve the automotive needs of a city of a million people. . . .

Liquid Hydrogen Is Dangerous

And once we obtain the liquid hydrogen for use in our cars, we're set then, right? Well, yes and no. Almost all existing gasoline engines can be easily converted to either natural gas or hydrogen fuels, and hydrogen-specific engines are easily engineered. [Car manufacturer] BMW has its 12-cylinder, 260-horsepower "Hydrogen 7" coupe in limited production. . . .

Road to Hydrogen Economy Long and Bumpy

When assessing the State of the Union in 2003, President Bush declared it was time to take a crucial step toward protecting our environment. He announced a $1.2 billion initiative to begin developing a national hydrogen infrastructure: a coast-to-coast network of facilities that would produce and distribute the hydrogen for powering hundreds of millions of fuel cell vehicles. Backed by a national commitment, he said, "our scientists and engineers will overcome obstacles to taking these cars from laboratory to showroom, so that the first car driven by a child born today could be powered by hydrogen, and pollution-free." With two years to go on the first, $720 million phase of the plan, PM [*Popular Mechanics*] asks that perennial question of every automotive journey: Are we almost there?

And the inevitable answer from the front seat: No. . . .

The Department of Energy projects the nation's consumption of fossil fuels will continue to rise—increasing 34 percent by 2030. When burned, these carbon-based fuels release millions of tons of carbon dioxide into the atmosphere, where the gas traps heat and is believed to contribute to global warming.

At first glance, hydrogen would seem an ideal substitute for these problematic fuels. Pound for pound, hydrogen contains almost three times as much energy as natural gas, and when consumed its only emission is pure, plain water. But unlike oil and gas, hydrogen is not a fuel. It is a way of storing or transporting energy. You have to make it before you can use it—generally by extracting hydrogen from fossil fuels, or by using electricity to split it from water.

And while oil and gas are easy to transport in pipelines and fuel tanks—they pack a lot of energy into a dense, stable form—hydrogen presents a host of technical and economic challenges. The lightest gas in the universe isn't easy to corral. . . .

Jeff Wise, "The Truth About Hydrogen,"
Popular Mechanics, *November 2006.*

111

The problem here is not power—as in the case of most hybrids—but fuel storage. Since hydrogen is considered in the National Electric Code to be second only to acetylene in explosive danger, it is likely that any production hydrogen-fueled vehicle would be built around protecting the fuel tank.

BMW elected to store the hydrogen fuel (costing in Germany the equivalent of about $10 per gallon of gasoline) as liquid hydrogen, known in the industry as LH_2.

Liquid hydrogen, being extremely cold, is touchy to work with. Having had some experience with cryogenics at NASA [National Aeronautics and Space Administration] in the '60s, I can personally attest that even handling liquid nitrogen, which at minus 320°F is 100 degrees "hotter" than LH_2, is tricky—and nitrogen is not explosive. Hydrogen fuel tanks must have a combination of vacuum barriers and "super-insulation"—usually multiple layers of aluminum foil and Mylar—and be constructed of materials that won't shatter like glass at ultra-cold temperatures. Fittings, seals, and valves are particularly difficult to manufacture and maintain.

And then there are the space requirements. Hydrogen as a liquid fuel requires 3.4 times the volume of an equivalent amount of gasoline. For a gasoline-powered car to have a range of 300 miles at 25 miles per gallon, a 12-gallon gasoline tank made of regular, un-insulated carbon steel would be required. To achieve the same range, a hydrogen-powered car would require a state-of-the-art cryogenic pressure vessel with a capacity of over 40 gallons, which would likely eliminate such luxuries as a trunk. The Hydrogen 7 holds about eight kilograms—or nine gallons—for a range of less than 70 miles. . . .

Fuel Cells Are Impractical

Then there are the other hydrogen engines, driven by fuel cells. In and of themselves, fuel cells are an almost ideal machine in that they have no major moving parts and are therefore incredibly reliable. When compressed hydrogen is used in them as a fuel, there are three outputs from the cell: electricity, heat, and water. With an efficiency of about 50 percent, half the energy from the hydrogen fuel is converted into electricity without the need for a generator.

However, while there is great enthusiasm for the hydrogen fuel cell for use in automobiles, this technology has been rightly called "the miracle that is always 10 years over the horizon." There are numerous problems, with cost being among the most serious. GM Vice President Larry Burns opined that the cost of fuel-cell vehicles must be reduced 90 percent to compete with internal combustion engines. One of the major cost factors is the significant amounts of platinum required as a catalyst for fuel-cell operation.

Another negative is the lack of an infrastructure to provide hydrogen. The "hydrogen fuel station" of the future would be more akin to docking at the International Space Station than today's pump-it-yourself and pay-at-the-pump operation. The hydrogen fuel station would have to have either an on-site electrolysis plant to produce the hydrogen—which would require major utility service—or giant high-pressure and/or cryogenic vessels to store the compressed or liquefied hydrogen. If stored at 13,000 psi [pounds per square inch], the volume required would be the same as for LH_2—3.4 times the space for the equivalent amount of gasoline.

Any fuel-cell-powered automobile would resemble today's battery-gasoline hybrids in terms of drivability, as the fuel cells do not come up to power instantaneously and don't have the output needed for bursts of power when accelerating to enter freeway traffic. But if the fuel-cell-powered plug-in car does not provide better drivability, why buy it? No less an unexpected critic than the Clinton administration's Department of Energy program manager Joseph Romm comments: "If you're going to the trouble of building a plug-in [car] and therefore have an electric drive train and a battery capable of storing a charge, then you could have a cheap gasoline engine along with you or an expensive fuel cell." Dr. Romm, whose Ph.D. in physics is from MIT, thinks that consumers will opt for the cheaper vehicle.

"A well-designed [hydrogen transition] can resolve most of the environmental problems of the current fossil-fuel system without making new ones, and can greatly enhance security."

Hydrogen Fuel Cells Are the Best Hope for the Future

Amory B. Lovins

In the following viewpoint, Amory B. Lovins argues that a future economy based on hydrogen fuel can provide important economic, environmental, and national security benefits. Lovins provides basic information about elemental hydrogen and its potential as an energy carrier. He offers reasons why the Rocky Mountain Institute, a nonprofit research center he co-founded, is optimistic about the transition to a hydrogen economy. Lovins is a physicist and CEO of the Rocky Mountain Institute.

As you read, consider the following questions:

1. Why does Lovins say hydrogen isn't an energy source?
2. According to Lovins, where do improvements need to be made before there can be a rapid and profitable transition to hydrogen?

3. What three obstacles to a hydrogen economy does Lovins think have been sufficiently resolved?

Hydrogen technologies are maturing. The world's existing hydrogen industry is starting to be recognized as big—producing one-fourth as much volume of gas each year as the global natural-gas industry. Industry, government, and civil society are becoming seriously engaged in designing a transition from refined petroleum products, natural gas, and electricity to hydrogen as the dominant way to carry, store, and deliver useful energy. New transitional paths are emerging, some with a vision across sectoral or disciplinary boundaries that makes them harder for specialists to grasp. Naturally, there's rising speculation about winners, losers, and hidden agendas. And as the novel hydrogen concept is overlaid onto longstanding and rancorous debates about traditional energy policy, constituencies are realigning in unexpected ways.

Start of the Hydrogen Era

In short, the customary wave of confusion is spreading across the country. What's this all about? Is hydrogen energy really a good idea? Is it just a way for incumbent industries to reinforce their dominance, or could it be a new, different, and hopeful melding of innovation with competition? Is it a panacea for humanity's energy predicament, or a misleading *deus ex machina* [savior] destined to inflict public disappointment and cynicism, or neither, or both?

The conversation about hydrogen is confused but hardly fanciful. The chairs of eight major oil and car companies have said the world is entering the oil endgame and the start of the Hydrogen Era. Royal Dutch/Shell's planning scenarios in 2001 envisaged a radical, China-led leapfrog to hydrogen (already underway): hydrogen would fuel a fourth of the vehicle fleet in the industrialized countries by 2025, when world oil use, stagnant meanwhile, would start to fall. President [George W.]

Bush's 2003 State of the Union message emphasized the commitment he'd announced a year earlier to develop hydrogen-fuel-cell cars. . . .

Yet many diverse authors have lately criticized hydrogen energy, some severely. Some call it a smokescreen to hide White House opposition to promptly raising car efficiency using conventional technology, or fear that working on hydrogen would divert effort from renewable energy sources. Some are skeptical of hydrogen because the President endorsed it, others because environmentalists did. Many wonder where the hydrogen will come from, and note that it's only as clean and abundant as the energy sources from which it's made. Most of the critiques reflect errors meriting a tutorial on basic hydrogen facts. . . .

Hydrogen Is a Versatile Energy Carrier

Hydrogen makes up about 75% of the known universe, but is not an energy *source* like oil, coal, wind, or sun. Rather, it is an energy *carrier* like electricity or gasoline—a way of transporting useful energy to users. Hydrogen is an especially versatile carrier because like oil and gas, but unlike electricity, it can be stored in large amounts (albeit often at higher storage cost than hydrocarbons [such as oil and gas]), and can be made from almost any energy source and used to provide almost any energy service. Like electricity, hydrogen is an extremely high-quality form of energy, and can be so readily converted to electricity and back that fuel-cell pioneer Geoffrey Ballard suggests they be thought of together as a fungible [interchangeable] commodity he calls "Hydricity™."

The reason hydrogen isn't an energy *source* is that it's almost never found by itself, the way oil and gas are. Instead, it must first be freed from chemical compounds in which it's bound up. There are broadly three ways to liberate hydrogen: using heat and catalysts to "reform" hydrocarbons or carbohydrates, or electricity to split ("electrolyze") water, or experimental processes, based typically on sunlight, plasma discharge, or microorganisms. All devices that produce hydrogen on a small scale, at or near the customer, are collectively called "hydrogen appliances" to distinguish them from traditional large-scale industrial production.

Hydrogen as Fuel

Fossil-fuel molecules are combinations of carbon, hydrogen, and various other atoms. Roughly two-thirds of the fossil-fuel atoms burned in the world today are hydrogen. (However, hydrogen yields a smaller share of fossil-fuel energy, because its chemical bonds are weaker than carbon's.) The debate is about whether combusting the last third of the fossil fuel—the carbon—is necessary; whether it might be cheaper and more attractive not to burn that carbon, but only to use the hydrogen; and to what degree that hydrogen should be replaced by hydrogen made with renewable energy sources.

Using hydrogen as a fuel, rather than burning fossil fuels directly, yields only water (and perhaps traces of nitrogen oxides if used in a high-temperature process). This can reduce pollution and climate change, depending on the source of the hydrogen. But when journalists write that hydrogen can "clean the air," that's shorthand for keeping pollutants out of the air, not removing those already there.

Hydrogen is the lightest element and molecule. Molecular hydrogen (two hydrogen atoms, H_2) is eight times lighter than natural gas. Per unit of energy contained, it weighs 64% less than gasoline or 61% less than natural gas: 1 kilogram (2.2 lb) of hydrogen has about the same energy as 1 U.S. gallon of gasoline, which weighs not 2.2 but 6.2 pounds. But the flip side of lightness is bulk. Per unit of *volume*, hydrogen gas contains only 30% as much energy as natural gas, both at atmospheric pressure. Even when hydrogen is compressed to 170 times atmospheric pressure (170 bar), it contains only 6% as much energy as the same volume of gasoline. Hydrogen is

Americans Support Hydrogen

A nationwide telephone survey of a representative cross-section of 1,004 adults, conducted June 17–20, 2005, explored Americans' attitudes toward U.S. energy policy and emerging automotive technologies. . . .

Support for Hydrogen: The public embraces the development of new technologies and alternative fuels that will produce more energy-efficient vehicles, and sees hydrogen fuel cell vehicles as the best solution to reducing gas consumption and emissions. For that reason, a majority favors government support of hydrogen development. Specifically:

- 79 percent of respondents described advances in automotive technology as "absolutely critical" or "very important."

- A plurality (29 percent) described hydrogen fuel cell-powered vehicles as those with the best chance for long-term success, compared to 23 percent for hybrids and 18 percent for traditional gas-powered engines.

- 65 percent of Americans believe that the U.S. government should make a major funding commitment to transform the auto industry from a gasoline-based system to a hydrogen-based system.

"GM Survey Finds Americans Support Energy Independence, Hydrogen-Based Economy," GM Inside News, June 29, 2005.

thus most advantageous where lightness is worth more than compactness, as is often true for mobility fuels.

Assessing Hydrogen's Price Not as Costly as It Seems

One of the biggest challenges of judging hydrogen's potential is how to compare it fairly and consistently with other energy carriers. Fossil fuels are traditionally measured in cost, volume, or mass per unit of *energy content*. That's valid only if the fuels being compared are all used in similar devices and at similar efficiencies, so all yield about the same amount of energy service. But that's not valid for hydrogen. Fuel cells. . .are not subject to the same thermodynamic limits as fuel-driven engines, because they're electrochemical devices, not heat engines. A hydrogen fuel-cell car can therefore convert hydrogen energy into motion about 2–3 times as efficiently as a normal car converts gasoline energy into motion: depending on how it's designed and run, a good fuel-cell system is about 50–70% efficient, hydrogen-to-electricity, while a typical car engine's efficiency from gasoline to output shaft averages only about 15–17% efficient. (Both systems then incur further minor losses to drive the wheels.) This means you can drive several times as far on a gallon-equivalent (in energy content) of hydrogen in a fuel-cell car as on a gallon of gasoline in an engine-driven car. Conversely, hydrogen costing several times as much as gasoline per unit of *energy contained* can thus cost the same *per mile* driven. Since you buy automotive fuel to get miles, not energy, ignoring such differences in end-use efficiency is a serious distortion, and accounts for much of the misinformation being published about hydrogen's high cost. Hydrogen's advantage in cars is especially large because cars run mainly at low loads, where fuel cells are most efficient and engines are least efficient. . . .

To reinforce this [last] point, the U.S. Department of Energy (DOE) says bulk hydrogen made and consumed onsite costs about $0.71/kg. That's equivalent in *energy* content to $0.72 per gallon of gasoline. But *per mile driven*—which is the objective—it's equivalent to about one-third to one-half that price, i.e., to about $0.24–0.36/gallon-equivalent, because of the 2–3-fold greater efficiency of a hydrogen fuel cell than a gasoline engine in running a car. Of course, the *price* of hydrogen *delivered* into the car's fuel tank will be much higher. For example, DOE says the delivered price of industrial liquid hydrogen is about \$2.20–3.10/kg. If it could be delivered into the tank of a car for the same price, it would be roughly equivalent *per mile* to \$1-a-gallon gasoline. Thus it can cost several times as much to deliver liquid hydrogen as to produce it. . . .Price also depends on hydrogen purity. So to assess hydrogen's price or cost or value or benefit meaningfully, we need to know how it'll be used, whether it's pure enough for the task, whether it's delivered to the task, and how much of the desired work it actually does. . . .

How to Launch the Hydrogen Transition

So much for the basics. What's different about Rocky Mountain Institute's [RMI] perspective that underlies this paper?

RMI believes that radical but practical and advantageous efficiency improvements at three levels—vehicles, energy distribution, and overall energy infrastructure—can make the hydrogen transition rapid and profitable.

At least for the next decade or two, RMI envisions a distributed model for hydrogen production and delivery that integrates the gas, electricity, building, and mobility infrastructures. Instead of building a costly new distribution infrastructure for hydrogen, we'd use excess capacity inherent in the existing gas and electricity distribution infrastructures, then make the hydrogen locally so it requires little or no further distribution. Only after this decentralized approach had built up a large hydrogen market in buildings and vehicles could centralized hydrogen production merit much investment, except in special circumstances.

RMI's insights into the full economic value of distributed power suggest that hydrogen fuel cells *today* can economically displace less efficient central resources for delivering electricity, paving the way for hydrogen use to spread rapidly, financed by its own revenues.

RMI recognizes that especially in North America, natural gas is logically the main near-term fuel to launch the hydrogen transition, along with cost-effective renewables. If making hydrogen requires more natural gas . . . , it should come first from natural gas saved by making existing applications more efficient. In the longer run, more mature and diverse renewables will play an important and ultimately a dominant role. Even during the initial, mainly fossil-fueled, stages of the hydrogen transition, carbon emissions will be much smaller than today's emissions from burning those fossil fuels directly. In time, those carbon emissions will approach zero. Insisting that they *start* at zero—that hydrogen be made solely from renewable energy sources, starting now—is making the perfect the enemy of the good. But done right, the hydrogen transition will actually make renewable energy more competitive and speed its adoption. . . .

Hydrogen Technology Is Ready

The oft-described technical obstacles to a hydrogen economy—storage, safety, and the cost of the hydrogen and its distribution infrastructure—have already been sufficiently resolved to support rapid deployment starting now. No technological breakthroughs are needed, although many will probably continue to occur. Until volume manufacturing of fuel cells starts in the next few years, even costly handmade or pilot-produced versions can already compete in substantial entry markets. Automotive use of fuel cells can flourish many years sooner if automakers adopt recent advances in crashworthy, cost-competitive ultralight autobodies. If fuel cells prove difficult to commercialize or hydrogen's benefits are desired sooner, there might even be a transitional role for hydrogen-fueled engine-hybrid vehicles.

The hydrogen transition should not need enormous investments in addition to those that the energy industries are already making. Instead, it will displace many of those investments. Hydrogen deployment may well need *less* net capital than business-as-usual, and should be largely self-financing from its revenues.

A well-designed hydrogen transition will also use little more, no more, or quite possibly *less* natural gas than business-as-usual.

A rapid hydrogen transition will probably be *more* profitable than business-as-usual for oil and car companies, and can quickly differentiate the business performance of early adopters.

Most of the hydrogen needed to displace the world's gasoline is already being produced for other purposes, including making gasoline. A hydrogen industry big enough to displace all gasoline, while sustaining the other industrial processes that now use hydrogen, would be only several-fold bigger than the mature hydrogen industry that exists today, although initially it will probably rely mainly on smaller units of production, nearer to their customers, to avoid big distribution costs.

A poorly designed hydrogen transition could cause environmental problems, but a well-designed one can resolve most of the environmental problems of the current fossil-fuel system without making new ones, and can greatly enhance security.

Periodical Bibliography

The following articles have been selected to supplement the diverse views presented in this chapter.

Joseph D'Agnese	"Falling in Love with Wind: How a Small Farm Town Traded Its Dairy Cows for Renewable Energy," *OnEarth*. Summer 2007.
Danny Duncan	"The Cult of Global Warming," *Sojourners Magazine*. September–October 2007.
Steve Heckeroth	"Solar Is the Solution," *Mother Earth News*. December 2007.
Michael K. Heiman and Barry D. Solomon	"Fueling U.S. Transportation: The Hydrogen Economy and Its Alternatives," *Environment*. October 2007.
Marianne Lavelle	"Getting a Second Wind," *U.S. News & World Report*. November 5, 2007.
Arthur Robinson and Noah Robinson	"Energy for America: We Can Achieve Energy Independence for the 21st Century Without Destroying the Environment," *The New American*. January 7, 2008.
ScienceDaily	"Renewable Energy Wrecks Environment, According to Researcher," July 25, 2007.
Dinesh C. Sharma	"Transforming Rural Lives Through Decentralized Green Power," *Futures*. June 2007.
Lisa Stiffler	"Clean vs. Dirty Is Only Part of Renewable Energy Debate," *Seattlepi.com*. October 30, 2006.
William Sweet	"Better Planet: Dirty Coal Plants Are Killers," *Discover*. August 2007.
Fareed Zakaria	"It's Not a Silver Bullet," *Newsweek*. November 5, 2007.

OPPOSING
VIEWPOINTS®
SERIES

CHAPTER 3

What Are the Benefits of Ethanol as a Renewable Transportation Fuel?

Chapter Preface

San Francisco, California, has a unique recycling program. The city collects restaurant grease. Turns out the greasy fryer remains from McDonald's or KFC are still useful. The city is going to use the old grease to make a kind of diesel fuel, aptly named biodiesel because it comes from agricultural processes rather than petroleum. Biodiesel, like ethanol, is a renewable fuel that can be used in diesel engines and many schools, universities, and communities are investing in it.

In November 2007, San Francisco launched *SFGreasecycle*, a program where the city picks up used cooking oil and grease from local restaurants, hotels, and other commercial food preparation establishments. Using a simple chemical process— one that is commonly performed in college organic chemistry classes—the city turns the oils into biodiesel. City officials say that this recycling program is beneficial not only because the resulting biodiesel can be used as fuel for city vehicles, but also because it keeps used grease from being illegally dumped into city sewers. According to the San Francisco Public Utilities Commission, grease congeals and clogs sewers and creates serious maintenance problems. Eventually, San Francisco wants to recycle the grease produced in homes and use the biodiesel to power the city's buses, fire trucks, and other vehicles.

Biodiesel is not new. In 1900, Rudolf Diesel demonstrated the engine named after him at the Paris World Exhibition. In that prototype engine he used peanut oil, the first biodiesel. For the next twenty years, diesel engines were powered by vegetable oils. However, in the 1920s, oil manufacturers, who were already producing gasoline, began producing a product specifically for the diesel engine. Using political and economic influences, the oil industry made petroleum-based diesel the fuel of choice for the diesel engine.

Pollution concerns about petroleum diesel fuel, tight petroleum supplies, and high prices have led to renewed interest in biodiesel. During the oil embargo in the 1970s (when Arab oil companies stopped exporting oil to countries that were supporting Israel in the Yom Kippur War, resulting in shortages) many people became interested in biodiesel. At that time, most of it was produced on a small scale. In the late 1990s, biodiesel started to be produced commercially—mostly from soybean oil. The National Biodiesel Board reported that 500,000 gallons of biodiesel were produced in 1999. In 2006, almost 250 million gallons of biodiesel were produced.

Liquid fuels produced from biomass are usually called "biofuels." (Biomass can be defined many ways but generally includes agricultural crops, trees, animal manure, and food processing waste.) Biodiesel, like ethanol (which today is primarily derived from corn), is touted as a renewable biofuel. Biodiesel is considered a renewable fuel because it is made from agricultural crops (soybean) or from food processing waste (restaurant grease). Ethanol and biodiesel are the two most prominent biofuels on the market.

Organizations such as the National Biodiesel Board (NBB) say that biodiesel is an environmentally friendly, economically beneficial alternative to petroleum-based diesel fuel. According to the NBB, biodiesel contains no sulfur or aromatic hydrocarbons, and use of biodiesel in a conventional diesel engine results in a substantial reduction of harmful tailpipe emissions. The organization also cites a U.S. Department of Energy study showing that the production and use of biodiesel, compared with petroleum diesel, results in a 78.5 percent reduction in carbon dioxide emissions. Using biodiesel, says the NBB, can help fight climate change. The NBB and the American Soybean Association say that using biodiesel can offset oil imports and enhance the nation's energy security. Furthermore, utilizing homegrown vegetable oil provides many economic benefits to small towns and rural communities across the United States.

Some people are concerned about the impacts of producing and using biodiesel. A report, published in 2008 by Friends of the Earth and several human rights groups, said that increasing demands for tropical palm oil for food and biofuels—particularly biodiesel—was causing millions of acres of forests to be cleared for plantations and destroying the livelihoods of indigenous peoples. Another 2008 study by the University of Minnesota and the Nature Conservancy found that the loss of carbon dioxide-absorbing trees resulting from the clearance of forests for biofuels production far outweighs any greenhouse gas savings that could come from using biofuels.

There are many sides to the biodiesel debate. The debate about ethanol, the other major biofuel today, is very similar to the biodiesel debate. In the following chapter, the authors provide their viewpoints on the benefits and costs of using ethanol as a renewable transportation fuel.

> *"Ethanol is earning increasing attention as a potentially cleaner, renewable, and domestically produced alternative to fossil fuels for transportation."*

Using Ethanol as Fuel Is Beneficial

Natural Resources Defense Council and Climate Solutions

In the following viewpoint, the Natural Resources Defense Council (NRDC) and Climate Solutions argue that ethanol, alcohol made from plants, is a good alternative to gasoline for the nation's transportation needs. The authors looked at ten different studies that attempted to quantify the energy return on investment of ethanol produced from corn and ethanol produced from cellulose (the fibrous component of woody plants and trees). Energy return on investment is an indicator of how much energy is consumed to make a fuel versus how much energy the fuel provides. The authors say that ethanol produced from corn or cellulose provides a good energy investment and reduces greenhouse gas emissions and negative land use. The NRDC is one of the largest environmental organizations in the United States. Climate Solutions is a nonprofit organization in the Pacific Northwest that finds solutions to global warming.

As you read, consider the following questions:

1. What percent of the world's total oil production do the authors claim is consumed by the United States? What percent of known oil reserves does the United States control?

2. According to the authors, how many gallons of corn ethanol did U.S. farmers produce in 2004? Was this a significant part of the corn harvest?

3. Why do the authors say that the measure of energy return on investment has quick appeal to policy makers?

A merica's dependence on nonrenewable energy sources threatens our security, economy, and environment. America consumes 25 percent of the world's total oil production, but controls only 3 percent of the world's known oil reserves. This means that we must pay high prices for oil imported from some of the most unstable regions of the world and suffer the environmental and public health consequences of our rampant oil consumption—polluted air, smog-filled cities, and the range of threats associated with global warming.

Similar environmental, health, and security concerns surround the other forms of nonrenewable energy. Coal power plants spew toxic emissions such as mercury and carbon dioxide into our air. Nuclear energy production brings national security concerns and uncertainty about how to safely manage the radioactive waste produced. And while natural gas offers a cleaner and safer alternative, like oil it is a finite resource, and much of the gas identified as technically recoverable is either uneconomic to exploit or located in places where its recovery would result in severe ecological damage.

In the face of these questions and concerns, ethanol is earning increasing attention as a potentially cleaner, renewable, and domestically produced alternative to fossil fuels for transportation. However, since ethanol came to national attention after the oil shocks of the 1970s, it has been plagued by questions about its ability to reduce our dependence on fossil fuels. To help resolve these questions, NRDC [Natural Resources Defense Council] and Climate Solutions commissioned the Institute for Lifecyle Environmental Assessment to review and compare several of the most influential studies examining how well ethanol leverages nonrenewable energy inputs to deliver renewable energy. For our survey, we chose the 10 most representative works from the U.S. research teams that have studied this issue in depth since 1990.

The full report has been submitted to a peer-reviewed journal, *Environmental Science and Technology*, for publication and should be available to the public in the next few months. In the meantime, this literature review provides a brief summary of our findings.

Our first task in this effort was to define the terms of the discussion. [Since the 1980s], questions about whether and to what extent ethanol could replace fossil fuels in the U.S. energy supply for transportation have been hotly debated in a variety of circles—scientific, political, agricultural, environmental—yet few uniformly defined terms of art have emerged. To compare the results of several studies, we first defined our terms and determined the methodology that we would use to convert the results of various studies into values that could be compared against one another.

For ethanol, the energy return on nonrenewable energy investment, or simply the energy return on investment, is the ratio of the total energy contained in a liter of ethanol to the nonrenewable energy consumed during production of the same amount of ethanol, including cultivating crops, transporting them, and converting them into ethanol. In this equation, if the energy in the ethanol is equal to the nonrenewable energy input to the production process, the energy return on investment value is 1. Values less than 1 mean that more nonrenewable energy was consumed during the production of ethanol than the amount of energy contained in the ethanol—a result that begs the question why not simply use the nonrenewable energy sources directly. Values greater than 1 mean that the ethanol contains more energy than the nonrenewable energy consumed in the manufacturing process—a result that indicates that ethanol successfully captures and delivers renewable energy and can indeed help us reduce our dependence on fossil fuels.

Corn Ethanol vs. Cellulosic Ethanol

There are two fundamentally different sources of ethanol: starch ethanol produced from the fruit and seeds of plants (for our purposes, corn ethanol produced from the kernels of corn) and cellulosic ethanol produced from whole plants—the leaves, stems, and stalks.

The production of corn ethanol in the United States has steadily increased over the last several years and 95 percent of all ethanol in the United States comes from corn. In 2004, farmers in the United States produced more than 3.4 billion gallons of corn ethanol, consuming 11 percent of the country's corn harvest. The technology for corn ethanol production can be considered mature as of the late 1980s. However, manufacturers continue to make improvements in process efficiency and farmers have reduced the amount of fertilizer required per bushel of corn produced. Taken together, these advancements will gradually decrease the amount of gross energy input to the corn ethanol manufacturing process over time.

Cellulosic ethanol, meanwhile, can be produced from a number of different crops. The manufacturing processes for this type of ethanol consume the entire plant, including lignin, a chemical compound found in the cell walls of plants that is combusted to fuel the industrial process. Cellulosic ethanol has never been manufactured on an industrial scale, and the technology to produce this type of ethanol is still being developed and is far from mature. Although the studies

Ethanol 101

- Auto manufacturers approve, and even recommend, fuel enriched with up to 10% ethanol for all cars.

- Flex-fuel vehicles are designed to run on E85 (85% ethanol and 15% gasoline)—the cleanest-burning, renewable fuel available today.

- By looking at your vehicle's fuel cap, you can tell if it's a flex-fuel vehicle—meaning it can run on regular gasoline, 10% ethanol-enriched fuel or E85.

- Fuel enriched with 10% ethanol is manufacturer-approved for use in small engines, including power equipment, motorcycles, snowmobiles, and outboard motors.

- Ethanol is the highest-performance fuel on the market, with an octane rating of 113 in its pure form.

- Ethanol-enriched fuel contains more oxygen—so it burns cleaner.

- Fuel enriched with 10% ethanol burns cleaner, helping to remove gummy deposits in the fuel system so engines can run with optimal performance.

- Enriching fuel with 10% ethanol helps it to burn cleaner and at a cooler temperature, which can add to engine longevity.

Ethanol Promotion and Information Council (EPIC),
"Ethanol Facts." www.drivingethanol.org.

discussed later in this paper show impressive energy returns on investment for cellulosic ethanol, further developed manufacturing processes for cellulosic ethanol could produce even greater renewable energy returns.

Corn Ethanol Studies

We reviewed six studies published since 1990 that examine the energy return on investment for corn ethanol. These included studies authored by Marland and Turhollow (1991), Lorenz and Morris (1995), Graboski (2002), Shapouri et al. (2002), Pimentel and Patkek (2005), and Kim and Dale (2005). We calculated the energy return on investment for each study ourselves, using the value of the nonrenewable energy input to the manufacturing process specified by the author of each study and a common total energy output value of 23.6 megajoules per liter of ethanol

Of the six studies that we compared, all but the Pimentel and Patkek study show renewable returns on nonrenewable energy investment for corn ethanol. Energy return on investment values for these five studies ranged from 1.29 to 1.65. The significantly lower energy return contained in the Pimentel and Patkek study can be attributed to a number of factors. First, Pimentel and Patkek reported significantly higher energy inputs to the agriculture, transport, industrial, and distribution components of the ethanol manufacturing process than any other research team over the last 15 years. Specifically, they reported approximately twice the electricity input in the industrial process compared to the other studies and nearly three times the energy input for feedstock transport. Pimentel and Patkek also reported two to three times more upstream energy inputs—energy used by the suppliers of commodities purchased by the farmer or ethanol manufacturer, such as nitrogen fertilizer—than the other studies. Additionally, they included upstream energy burdens not included in the other studies, such as personal energy consumption by laborers and the energy costs of manufacturing capital equipment. Excepting Pimentel and Patkek as an outlier [a result that lies so far outside the rest of the data it is often excluded], the energy return on investment values produced in the five other studies indicate that corn ethanol has a solid renewable energy return on its fossil energy investment—its use does indeed help reduce our fossil fuel consumption.

Cellulosic Ethanol Studies

We reviewed four studies published since 1990 that examine the energy return on investment for cellulosic ethanol. These included studies authored by Tyson et al. (1993), Lynd and Wang (2004), Sheehan et al. (2004), and Pimentel and Patkek (2005). Similar to our review and comparison of the corn ethanol studies discussed above, we calculated energy return on investment of ethanol ourselves, using the nonrenewable energy input value specified by the authors of each study and a common energy output value per liter of ethanol. In contrast to the corn ethanol studies, where all researchers modeled starch ethanol manufactured from corn, the research teams in these studies each modeled different crops.

Of the four studies we reviewed and compared, again all but the Pimentel and Patkek study show substantial renewable returns on nonrenewable energy investment to the production process. Energy return on investment values for these three studies ranged from 4.40 to 6.61, significantly higher than the energy return from corn ethanol. The wide variance of these numbers is consistent with the developing nature of cellulosic ethanol technology and the wide variety of feedstocks [crops from which ethanol is made] available. The significantly lower renewable energy return contained in the Pimentel and Patkek study can be attributed to these researchers' assumption that the industrial energy for manufacturing ethanol would be produced by fossil fuels and grid electricity, rather than by combustion of the lignin that comes to the production facility as part of the crop. All well-developed models of cellulosic ethanol production assume that industrial energy will be produced by lignin combustion—in fact, in most models the heat released by lignin combustion actually exceeds the heat required by the industrial process and can be used to generate surplus electricity.

Though manufacturing processes for cellulosic ethanol are not yet mature, the initial energy return on investment values are very encouraging, and the potential exists for even greater renewable energy returns as the technology continues to develop. Indeed, some analysts believe that energy return for mature cellulosic ethanol technology processes could exceed 10.

Policy Discussion

The energy return on investment measure had quick appeal to policymakers because it provides a straightforward and easily understood threshold value that can be used to gauge the benefit of ethanol production: energy return values greater than 1 mean that using ethanol results in reduced fossil fuel use; values less than 1 indicate that using ethanol would actually increase our fossil fuel use. However, this view oversimplifies the broader worth of biofuels production and use. A full understanding of the role that biofuels such as ethanol might play in America's energy future needs to take into account the relationship of biofuels to the environmental, social, and economic goals of our time. For instance, while energy return on investment does shed some light on a fuel's impacts on greenhouse gas emissions, it tells us nothing about the impacts of oil dependence or land use. Even within greenhouse gas emissions the picture is not as simple as it seems.

Greenhouse Gas Emissions

Coal has approximately 19 percent more carbon per unit of energy contained in the fuel than oil, whereas natural gas contains about 33 percent less. This means that if coal were used to produce ethanol, ethanol would have to have a better energy return on investment than gasoline—the main fossil fuel it would replace—to produce a net reduction in carbon dioxide emissions regardless. (Gasoline has an energy return on investment of 0.76.) Fortunately, most ethanol is produced using natural gas, and these facilities could actually have a lower energy return than gasoline and still produce a net reduction in carbon dioxide emissions. However, carbon dioxide is only one greenhouse gas; agricultural processes can induce methane and nitrous oxide, both potent greenhouse gases. . . .Thus, a more complete examination of the impact of ethanol production on greenhouse gas reduction must include an evaluation of the amount of each gas produced under each fuel scenario—gasoline, corn ethanol and cellulosic ethanol. Still, [this]. . .does indicate that ethanol production can reduce carbon dioxide emissions and that different production methods can produce greater or lesser greenhouse gas emissions.

Because the energy return on investment by itself does not indicate what type of nonrenewable energy is being invested in a process, this metric alone also paints an incomplete picture of ethanol's contribution to reducing our dependence on oil specifically. Fortunately, two of the corn ethanol studies in particular (Graboski and Shapouri et al.) took the additional step of estimating the reduction in crude oil consumption achieved by driving the same distance using ethanol versus gasoline. These studies show that very little petroleum is used in the production process of ethanol and thus a shift from gasoline to ethanol will reduce our oil dependence regardless of its impacts on our use of other fossil fuels.

Land Use

Land use arguably is the greatest environmental impact of ethanol production. A sustainable increase in land use to grow the plants used in ethanol may benefit the U.S. agricultural economy. However, too great an increase in land use could damage the landscape and ecosystems, and in countries with less available farmland than the United States, could compete with land needed for food production. Unfortunately, energy return on investment of ethanol gives us little insight into whether large-scale ethanol production will benefit or harm the U.S. agricultural economy, landscape, or ecosystems. Broadly, we can assume that the higher the renewable energy returns on investment of ethanol for a particular type of ethanol or technology for ethanol manufacture, the less additional land consumed by the manufacture of that ethanol. However, a more meaningful evaluation of the environmental-social interaction of ethanol production and land use requires a more sophisticated analysis of the relationship, such as land area per liter of ethanol.

Conclusion

Our analysis determined that both corn and cellulosic ethanol production return renewable energy on their fossil energy investments, though the results indicate that cellulosic ethanol production will be preferable to corn ethanol production. On the surface, cellulosic ethanol simply delivers profoundly more renewable energy than corn ethanol. And considered more closely across the social, economic, and environmental factors beyond simple energy return on investment, cellulosic ethanol production promises to consume less petroleum, produce fewer greenhouse gases, and require less land compared to corn ethanol. However, the corn ethanol industry is the foundation from which a much larger biofuels economy will grow. As the energy return on investment shows, corn ethanol is providing important fossil fuel savings and greenhouse gas emissions reductions today, and it is providing an even bigger oil savings.

> *"More smog, infinitely worse gas mileage, huge problems in distribution, and skyrocketing prices for gasoline. Maybe now that we're witnessing the third act in America's ethanol play, the upcoming epilogue will close this show forever."*

Using Ethanol as Fuel Is Not Beneficial

Ed Wallace

In the following viewpoint, Ed Wallace discounts the value of ethanol as a fuel. Wallace contends that the U.S. government has been trying to sell ethanol to the American public since the 1970s and with disastrous results. He maintains that ethanol is not green and is not cheap, as its supporters often claim. Wallace, an automotive expert, has a weekly column in the Fort Worth Star-Telegram *and is a contributing writer for* Business-Week *online.*

As you read, consider the following questions:

1. What was the Clean Air Act and how does Wallace say it is related to ethanol production in the United States?

2. How much did a barrel of oil cost in the year 2000?

3. According to Wallace, what key factor have studies ignored when assessing the energy conversion rate for ethanol-blended gasoline?

If there were ever a time when the truth in advertising standards should be put back into place, it's now—during the current (third) attempt to convince the public that the massive use of corn-derived ethanol [alcohol fuel] in our gasoline supply will alleviate our need for foreign oil. Ultimately, the answer to just one question determines ethanol's actual usefulness as a gasoline extender: "If the government hadn't mandated this product, would it survive in a free market?" Doubtful—but the misinformation superhighway has been rerouted to convince the public its energy salvation is at hand.

Government Supports Ethanol in 1970s and 1980s

The use of ethanol to reduce our dependence on foreign oil is nothing new. We also considered it during our nation's Project Independence in 1974, the year after the first Arab oil embargo. After the second energy crisis in 1979, an income tax credit of 40 cents per gallon of 190-proof ethanol produced was instituted as an incentive for refiners of ethanol to blend this product into gasoline.

Because this federal largesse [generosity] now existed, within five years, 163 ethanol plants had been built—but only 74 of them were still in operation. As gasoline availability opened up in the 1980s and gas prices went down, many ethanol plants simply went out of business.

Shortly thereafter, in yet another attempt to broaden the product's usage, Congress enacted a law that allowed car manufacturers to take excess mileage credits on any vehicle they built that was capable of burning an 85% blend of ethanol, better known as E85. General Motors took advantage of the credits, building relatively large volumes of the Suburban as a certified E85 vehicle. Although in real life that generation of the Suburban got less than 15 mpg, the credits it earned GM against its Corporate Average Fuel Economy (CAFE) ratings meant that on paper, the Suburban delivered more than 29 mpg.

Other manufacturers also built E85-capable vehicles—one such car was the Ford Taurus. Congress may have intended simply to create a market for this particular fuel by having these vehicles available for sale. But what the excess mileage credits actually did was save Detroit millions each year in penalties it would have owed for not meeting the CAFE regulations' mileage standards.

Despite Association with Smog, EPA Backs Ethanol in 1990s

In the mid-'90s the Clean Air Act of 1990 kicked in, mandating that a reformulated gasoline be sold in the nation's smoggiest cities. So the Clinton Administration again tried to create an ethanol industry in America, by having the Environmental Protection Agency [EPA] mandate that fully 30% of the oxygenates [compounds like ethanol that reduce carbon monoxide emissions, one of the ingredients of smog] to be used in gasoline under that program come from a renewable source. But members of the American Petroleum Institute had already geared up for the production of Methyl Tertiary Butyl Ether (MTBE), their oxygenate of choice. The ensuing lawsuit was argued before the Court of Appeals for the District of Columbia on February 16, 1995.

The EPA took the position that it had been given a mandate to find ways to conserve the nation's fossil-fuel reserves, so it needed a renewable fuel—and ethanol neatly fit that bill. But there were problems with that argument, not least of which was the fact that the judges could find no charter or mandate from Congress that gave the EPA the statutory right to do anything about fossil fuel, reserves or otherwise.

Even more damaging, the EPA's own attorney admitted to the judges that because of its higher volatility, putting ethanol into the nation's fuel supply would likely increase smog where it was used. One of the judges, on hearing that the EPA was actively promoting a substance that could in fact diminish air quality, wondered aloud, "Is the EPA in outer space?"

The final decision favored the American Petroleum Institute. The judges agreed that the EPA was bound by law only to promote items that would improve air quality—not to reverse the nation's advances in smog reduction. That decision was apparently forgotten with record speed. In the summer of 2000, ethanol as an additive was mandated for the upper Midwest, including the city of Chicago and parts of the state of Wisconsin.

Prices for Ethanol-Blended Gas Soared in 2000

After Asian economies had collapsed in the late '90s, the price of oil had fallen to as low as $10 a barrel. Gasoline was selling in many parts of the U.S. for as little as 99 cents a gallon. But by 2000, the per-barrel price had risen to $32, and gas was averaging $1.55 a gallon nationally. . . .The nation's drivers were incensed by the rising prices of gasoline and oil. And then reformulated gasoline made with ethanol hit Chicago and points north. Gas prices there suddenly soared over $2.00, with a few stations selling their product for as much as $2.54 per gallon.

At some stations in southeast Wisconsin, where reformulated gasoline wasn't required and gas cost considerably less, pumps ran dry in the panic, as savvy consumers topped off their tanks. Citing [a survey], the Associated Press on June 12, 2000, stated, "Dealers in the Midwest, where many cities use a reformulated gas blended with the corn derivative ethanol, are paying a premium at wholesale."

Everyone Loves Ethanol, Except Taxpayers

Ethanol is not much used in Europe, but it is a fuel additive in the U.S., and a growing number of cars can use either gasoline or ethanol. It accounted for only around 3.5 percent of U.S. fuel consumption last year, but production is growing by 25 percent a year because the government subsidizes domestic production *and* penalizes imports. As a result, refineries are popping up like mushrooms all over the Midwest, which sees itself as the Texas of green fuel.

Why is the government so generous? Because ethanol is just about the only alternative-energy initiative that has broad political support. Farmers love it because it provides a new source of subsidy. Hawks love it because it offers the possibility that the U.S. may wean itself off Middle Eastern oil.

The automotive industry loves it, because switching to a green fuel will take the global-warming heat off cars. The oil industry loves it because ethanol as a fuel additive means it is business as usual for the time being.

Taxpayers seem not to have noticed they are footing the bill.

"Corn-Based Ethanol Not Cheap, Not Green,"
The Economist, *April 11, 2007.*

Just a few months later, Brazil—which had worked toward energy independence since the mid-'70s oil crisis and had already mandated that the percentage of ethanol in its fuel be raised to 24%—was forced to import ethanol refined by the [U.S.-based] Archer Daniels Midland Co. when the nation's sugar-cane crop suffered a devastating drought. Brazil understood that a year of poor crops was just as damaging to its national fuel supply as Iran taking its oil off-market would be to the rest of the world.

Then came the third act in this ethanol play—and possibly the most misleading and disingenuous PR [public relations] campaign ever.

Ethanol Not Green or Cheap

It started with Congress, which mandated that even more ethanol be used to extend the nation's fuel supply. From General Motors, an ad campaign called "Live Green, Go Yellow" gave America the impression that by purchasing GM vehicles capable of using E85 ethanol, we could help reduce our dependence on foreign oil.

What GM left out of its ads was that the use of this fuel would likely increase the amount of smog during the summer months (as the EPA's own attorneys had admitted in 1995)—and that using E85 in GM products would lower their fuel efficiency by as much as 25%. (*USA Today*. . .reported [in 2006] that the U.S. Department of Energy estimated the drop in mileage at 40%.)

But one final setup for the public has gone unnoticed. At the Web site www.fueleconomy.gov, which confirms the 25% to 30% drop in mileage resulting from the use of this blended fuel, another feature lets users calculate and compare annual fuel costs using regular gasoline to costs using E85.

But the government site's automatic calculations are based on E85 selling for 37 cents per gallon less than regular gasoline, when the *USA Today* article reports that at many stations in the Midwest E85 is actually selling for 13 cents per gallon more than ordinary gas. Using the corrected prices for both gasoline and E85, the annual cost of fueling GM's Suburban goes from $2,709 to $3,763. Hence the suggestion that truth in advertising should come back into play. Possibly GM could rename this ad campaign "Shell Out Green, Turn Yellow."

Inefficient Ethanol

The other negative aspect of this inefficient fuel is that numerous studies have found that ethanol creates less energy than is required to make it. Other studies have found that ethanol creates "slightly" more energy than is used in its production. Yet not one of these studies takes into account that when E85 is used, the vehicle's fuel efficiency drops by at least 25%—and possibly by as much as 40%. Using any of the accredited studies as a baseline in an energy-efficiency equation, ethanol when used as a fuel is a net energy waste.

Furthermore, no one has even considered the severe disruption in the nation's fuel distribution that mandating a move into ethanol would cause. [In the spring of 2006], gas stations from Dallas to Philadelphia and parts of Massachusetts. . .had their tanks run dry due to a lack of ethanol to blend. The newswires have been filled with stories bemoaning the shortage of trucks, drivers, railcars, and barges to ship the product. Ethanol can't be blended at refineries and pumped through the nation's gasoline pipelines.

The. . .price spikes for gasoline have forcibly reminded the people of Chicago and Wisconsin of what happened when ethanol was forced on them during the summer of 2000. Moreover, the promise of energy independence that Brazil has explored through ethanol is widely misunderstood. Recently a Brazilian official, commenting on our third and most recent attempted conversion to ethanol, said that when Brazil tried using agricultural crops for ethanol, it achieved only a 1:1.20 energy conversion rate, too low to be worth the effort.

Close the Ethanol Show

On the other hand, ethanol from sugar cane delivered 1:8 energy conversion, which met the national mandate. Unfortunately for us, sugar cane isn't a viable crop in the climate of our nation's heartland. But the part of Brazil's quest for energy independence that the media usually overlooks is that ethanol wasn't the only fuel source the country was working on: Its other, more important, thrust was to find more oil. To that end, [in April 2006] Brazil's P50 offshore oil platform was turned on. Its anticipated daily output is high enough to make Brazil totally oil independent.

More smog, infinitely worse gas mileage, huge problems in distribution, and skyrocketing prices for gasoline. Maybe now that we're witnessing the third act in America's ethanol play, the upcoming epilogue will close this show forever. Even great advertising works only if the product does.

"The arguments in favor of cellulosic ethanol as a replacement for gasoline in cars and trucks are compelling."

Producing Ethanol from Cellulose Is Beneficial

Diane Greer

In the following viewpoint, Diane Greer asserts that cellulosic ethanol has the potential to reduce the nation's gasoline consumption. Greer discusses the main differences between ethanol made from corn and ethanol made from cellulosic biomass, such as agricultural and industrial waste. She concludes that with technological innovation, cellulosic ethanol can reduce greenhouse gas emissions, reduce the nation's dependence on foreign oil, and increase our energy security. Diane Greer is a writer and researcher specializing in sustainable business, green building, and alternative energy.

As you read, consider the following questions:

1. Why does Greer think cellulosic ethanol is better than corn ethanol?
2. What are polysaccharides, and what does Greer say is locked in them?

Diane Greer, "Creating Cellulosic Ethanol: Spinning Straw Into Fuel," *Biocycle*, April 2005, p. 61. www.harvestcleanenergy.org. Copyright © 2005 JG Press Inc. All rights reserved. Reproduced by permission.

3. According to Greer, what currently happens to agricultural residues?

In the Grimm Brothers' fairy tale, Rumpelstiltskin spins straw into gold. Thanks to advances in biotechnology, researchers can now transform straw, and other plant wastes, into "green" gold—cellulosic ethanol. While chemically identical to ethanol produced from corn or soybeans, cellulose ethanol exhibits a net energy content three times higher than corn ethanol and emits a low net level of greenhouse gases. Recent technological developments are not only improving yields but also driving down production cost, bringing us nearer to the day when cellulosic ethanol could replace expensive, imported "black gold" with a sustainable, domestically produced biofuel.

Cellulosic ethanol has the potential to substantially reduce our consumption of gasoline. "It is at least as likely as hydrogen to be an energy carrier of choice for a sustainable transportation sector," say the Natural Resources Defense Council (NRDC) and the Union of Concerned Scientists in a joint statement. Major companies and research organizations are also realizing the potential. Shell Oil has predicted "the global market for biofuels such as cellulosic ethanol will grow to exceed $10 billion by 2012." A [2004] study funded by the Energy Foundation and the National Commission on Energy Policy, entitled "Growing Energy: How Biofuels Can Help End America's Oil Dependence," concluded "biofuels coupled with vehicle efficiency and smart growth could reduce the oil dependency of our transportation sector by two-thirds by 2050 in a sustainable way."

Isn't All Ethanol the Same?

Conventional ethanol and cellulosic ethanol are the same product, but are produced utilizing different feedstocks and processes. Conventional ethanol is derived from grains such as corn and wheat or soybeans. Corn, the predominant feedstock, is converted to ethanol in either a dry or wet milling process. In dry milling operations, liquefied corn starch is produced by heating corn meal with water and enzymes. A second enzyme converts the liquefied starch to sugars, which are fermented by yeast into ethanol and carbon dioxide. Wet milling operations separate the fiber, germ (oil), and protein from the starch before it is fermented into ethanol.

Cellulosic ethanol can be produced from a wide variety of cellulosic biomass feedstocks including agricultural plant wastes (corn stover, cereal straws, sugarcane bagasse), plant wastes from industrial processes (sawdust, paper pulp) and energy crops grown specifically for fuel production, such as switchgrass. Cellulosic biomass is composed of cellulose, hemicellulose and lignin, with smaller amounts of proteins, lipids (fats, waxes and oils) and ash. Roughly, two-thirds of the dry mass of cellulosic materials are present as cellulose and hemicellulose. Lignin makes up the bulk of the remaining dry mass.

Unlocking the Sugars from Cellulosic Biomass

As with grains, processing cellulosic biomass aims to extract fermentable sugars from the feedstock. But the sugars in cellulose and hemicellulose are locked in complex carbohydrates called polysaccharides (long chains of monosaccharides or simple sugars). Separating these complex polymeric structures into fermentable sugars is essential to the efficient and economic production of cellulosic ethanol.

Two processing options are employed to produce fermentable sugars from cellulosic biomass. One approach utilizes acid hydrolysis to break down the complex carbohydrates into simple sugars. An alternative method, enzymatic hydrolysis, utilizes pretreatment processes to first reduce the size of the material to make it more accessible to hydrolysis. Once pretreated, enzymes are employed to convert the cellulosic biomass to fermentable sugars. The final step involves microbial fermentation yielding ethanol and carbon dioxide.

Cellulosic Ethanol Substantially Reduces Greenhouse Gas Emissions

Grain based ethanol utilizes fossil fuels to produce heat during the conversion process, generating substantial greenhouse gas emissions. Cellulosic ethanol production substitutes biomass for fossil fuels, changing the emissions calculations, according to Michael Wang of Argonne National Laboratories. Wang has created a "Well to Wheel" (WTW) life cycle analysis model to calculate greenhouse gas emissions produced by fuels in internal combustion engines. Life cycle analyses look at the environmental impact of a product from its inception to the end of its useful life.

"The WTW model for cellulosic ethanol showed greenhouse gas emission reductions of about 80% [over gasoline]," said Wang. "Corn ethanol showed 20 to 30% reductions." Cellulosic ethanol's favorable profile stems from using lignin, a biomass by-product of the conversion operation, to fuel the process. "Lignin is a renewable fuel with no net greenhouse gas emissions," explains Wang. "Greenhouse gases produced by the combustion of biomass are offset by the CO_2 [carbon dioxide] absorbed by the biomass as it grows."

Cellulosic Ethanol Can Be Produced from Many Different Feedstocks

Feedstock sources and supplies are another important factor differentiating the two types of ethanol. Agricultural wastes are a largely untapped resource. This low cost feedstock is more abundant and contains greater potential energy than simple starches and sugars. Currently, agricultural residues are plowed back into the soil, composted, burned or disposed in

Government Investing Millions in Cellulosic Ethanol

U.S. Department of Energy (DOE) Secretary Samuel W. Bodman. . .announced that DOE will invest up to $385 million for six biorefinery projects [from 2007 to 2010]. When fully operational, the biorefineries are expected to produce more than 130 million gallons of cellulosic ethanol per year. This production will help further President [George W.] Bush's goal of making cellulosic ethanol cost-competitive with gasoline by 2012 and, along with increased automobile fuel efficiency, reduce America's gasoline consumption by 20 percent [by 2017].

"These biorefineries will play a critical role in helping to bring cellulosic ethanol to market, and teaching us how we can produce it in a more cost effective manner," Secretary Bodman said. "Ultimately, success in producing inexpensive cellulosic ethanol could be a key to eliminating our nation's addiction to oil. By relying on American ingenuity and on American farmers for fuel, we will enhance our nation's energy and economic security."

"DOE Selects Six Cellulosic Ethanol Plants for up to $385 Million in Federal Funding," U.S. Department of Energy, February 28, 2007. www.energy.gov.

landfills. As an added benefit, collection and sale of crop residues offer farmers a new source of income from existing acreage.

Industrial wastes and municipal solid waste (MSW) can also be used to produce ethanol. Lee Lynd, an engineering professor at Dartmouth, has been working with the Gorham Paper Mill to convert paper sludge to ethanol. "Paper sludge is a waste material that goes into landfills at a cost of $80/dry ton," says Lynd. "This is genuinely a negative cost feedstock. And it is already pretreated, eliminating a step in the conversion process."...

Perennial grasses, such as switchgrass, and other forage crops are promising feedstocks for ethanol production. "Environmentally switchgrass has some large benefits and the potential for productivity increases," says John Sheehan of the National Renewable Energy Laboratory (NREL). The perennial grass has a deep root system, anchoring soils to prevent erosion and helping to build soil fertility. "As a native species, switchgrass is better adapted to our climate and soils," adds Nathanael Greene, NRDC Senior Policy Analyst. "It uses water efficiently, does not need a lot of fertilizers or pesticides and absorbs both more efficiently."

Technological Progress

Reducing the cost and improving the efficiency of separating and converting cellulosic materials into fermentable sugars is one of the keys to a viable industry. "On the technology side, we need a major push on overcoming the recalcitrance of biomass," continues Greene, referring to the difficulty in breaking down complex cellulosic biomass structures. "This is the greatest difficulty in converting biomass into fuel." R&D [research and development] efforts are focusing on the development of cost-effective biochemical hydrolysis and pretreatment processes. Technological advances promise substantially lower processing costs in these fields compared to acid hydrolysis. "In the enzyme camp, we have only scratched the surface of the potential of biotechnology to contribute to this area," adds Reade Dechton of Energy Futures Coalition. "We are at the very beginning of dramatic cost improvements."...

The arguments in favor of cellulosic ethanol as a replacement for gasoline in cars and trucks are compelling. Cellulosic ethanol will reduce our dependence on imported oil, increase our energy security and reduce our trade deficit. Rural economies will benefit in the form of increased incomes and jobs. Growing energy crops and harvesting agricultural residuals are projected to increase the value of farm crops, potentially eliminating the need for some agricultural subsidies. Finally, cellulosic ethanol provides positive environmental benefits in the form of reductions in greenhouse gas emissions and air pollution.

More Funding Needed

There is a growing consensus on the steps needed for biofuels to succeed: increased spending on R&D in conversion and processing technologies, funding for demonstration projects and joint investment or other incentives to spur commercialization. "If you do not do all three of these pieces, the effort is likely to stall," said Greene. "The challenge is to be really focused and make the commitment to make biofuels a part of our economy. We need to make these technologies work."

There is also agreement on one of the main factors impeding the development of biofuels—inadequate government funding. "We are grossly underinvesting in this area," says Dechton. "We are piddling along at 30 or 40 million dollars per year. This is a national security issue." Sheehan agrees, adding "the other problem is over the last several years Congressional earmarking has been horrendous. It is splintering critical resources, as a result effectiveness is way down. We do not have well aligned, consistently directed R&D effort."

The "Growing Energy" report calls for $2 billion in funding for cellulosic biofuels over the next ten years, with $1.1 billion directed at research, development and demonstration projects and the remaining [approximately] $800 million slated for the deployment of biorefineries. Other advocated subsidies and incentives for the industry include production tax credits, bond insurance for feedstock sellers and biofuels purchasers and efficacy insurance. "We would like to see private insurance but lacking private sector involvement, government should offer the insurance," said Greene. "The idea has two features, the amount of money available goes down over time, so by 2015 the industry is ready to stand on its own two feet and, second, the dollars available to developers is in a menu format. We will let them pick subsidies that work best for their product."

Biofuels Can Be Competitive

Given sufficient investment in research, development, demonstration and deployment, the report projects biorefineries producing cellulosic ethanol at a cost leaving the plant between $.59–$.91 per gallon by 2015. The price range is dependent upon plant scale and efficiency factors. At these prices, biofuels would be competitive with the wholesale price of gasoline.

In the past, discussions regarding ethanol as a potential replacement for gasoline have centered on the availability of suitable land in addition to a feed versus fuel debate. Technological and process advances coupled with the promise of biorefineries are allowing us to refocus the debate. Scenarios exist where well directed public policies emphasizing biofuels investment and incentives in addition to fuel efficiency could promote a transition to cellulosic ethanol. Given the right policy choices, America's farmers could one day be filling both our refrigerators and our gas tanks.

"No wonder many of the issues with cellulosic ethanol aren't discussed—there's no way to express the problems in a sound bite."

Producing Ethanol from Cellulose Is Not Beneficial

Alice Friedemann

In the following viewpoint, Alice Friedemann contends that producing significant quantities of cellulosic ethanol, as the United States government calls for, is neither beneficial nor sustainable. Friedemann believes that there are far too many problems associated with cellulosic ethanol, such as a negative energy balance and adverse impacts to fertile topsoil, for it ever to be viable. Alice Friedemann is a journalist specializing in energy issues.

As you read, consider the following questions:

1. According to Friedemann, how much of the nation's energy needs does the U.S. Department of Energy hope to supply in the form of biomass by 2030?

2. What is "EROEI"? What is the EROEI for cellulosic ethanol, according to researcher John Benemann?

Alice Friedemann, "Peak Soil: Why Cellulosic Ethanol, Biofuels, Are Not Sustainable and Are a Threat to America's National Security," *Culture Change*, April 10, 2007. www.culturechange.org. Reproduced by permission.

3. Why are scientists who study biofuels interested in termites?

Ethanol is an agribusiness get-rich-quick scheme that will bankrupt our topsoil.

Nineteenth-century western farmers converted their corn into whiskey to make a profit. Archer Daniels Midland (ADM), a large grain processor, came up with the same scheme in the 20th century. But ethanol was a product in search of a market, so ADM spent three decades relentlessly lobbying for ethanol to be used in gasoline. Today ADM makes record profits from ethanol sales and government subsidies.

The Department of Energy (DOE) hopes to have biomass supply 5% of the nation's power, 20% of transportation fuels, and 25% of chemicals by 2030. These combined goals are 30% of the current petroleum consumption.

Biomass Fuels Won't Get Off the Ground

Fuels made from biomass are a lot like the nuclear powered airplanes the Air Force tried to build from 1946 to 1961, for billions of dollars. They never got off the ground. The idea was interesting—atomic jets could fly for months without refueling. But the lead shielding to protect the crew and several months of food and water was too heavy for the plane to take off. The weight problem, the ease of shooting this behemoth down, and the consequences of a crash landing were so obvious, it's amazing the project was ever funded, let alone kept going for 15 years.

Biomass fuels have equally obvious and predictable reasons for failure. [Ecologist Howard] Odum says that time explains why renewable energy provides such low energy yields compared to non-renewable fossil fuels. The more work left to nature, the higher the energy yield, but the longer the time required. Although coal and oil took millions of years to form into dense, concentrated solar power, all we had to do was extract and transport them.

Cellulosic Ethanol Could Destroy Fertile Soil

With every step required to transform a fuel into energy, there is less and less energy yield. For example, to make ethanol from corn grain, which is how all U.S. ethanol is made now, corn is first grown to develop hybrid seeds, which next season are planted, harvested, delivered, stored, and preprocessed to remove dirt. Dry-mill ethanol is milled, liquefied, heated, saccharified, fermented, evaporated, centrifuged, distilled, scrubbed, dried, stored, and transported to customers. . . .

Fertile soil will be destroyed if crops and other "wastes" are removed to make cellulosic ethanol.

"We stand, in most places on earth, only six inches from desolation, for that is the thickness of the topsoil layer upon which the entire life of the planet depends," [said agricultural expert R. Neil Sampson in 1981].

Loss of topsoil has been a major factor in the fall of civilizations. You end up with a country like Iraq, formerly Mesopotamia, where 75% of the farm land became a salty desert.

Fuels from biomass are not sustainable, are ecologically destructive, have a net energy loss, and there isn't enough biomass in America to make significant amounts of energy because essential inputs like water, land, fossil fuels, and phosphate ores are limited. . . .

Cellulose Perfected over Hundreds of Millions of Years

Many plants want animals to eat their seeds and fruit to disperse them. Some seeds only germinate after going through an animal gut and coming out in ready-made fertilizer. Seeds and fruits are easy to digest compared to the rest of the plant, that's why all of the commercial ethanol and biodiesel are made from the yummy parts of plants, the grain, rather than the stalks, leaves, and roots.

But plants don't want to be entirely devoured. They've spent hundreds of millions of years perfecting structures that

Cellulosic Ethanol Even Worse Than Corn Ethanol

Up-to-date analysis of the 14 energy inputs that typically go into corn production and the 9 invested in fermentation and distillation operations confirms that 29 percent more energy (derived from fossil fuels) is required to produce a gallon of corn ethanol than is contained in the ethanol. Ethanol from cellulosic biomass is worse: With current technology, 50 percent more energy is required to produce a gallon than the product can deliver.

David Pimentel and Tad Patkek,
"Green Plants, Fossil Fuels, and Now Biofuels,"
BioScience, *November 2006.*

can't easily be eaten. Be thankful plants figured this out, or everything would be mown down to bedrock.

If we ever did figure out how to break down cellulose in our back yard stills, it wouldn't be long before the 6.5 billion people on the planet destroyed the grasslands and forests of the world to power generators and motorbikes.

Don Augenstein and John Benemann, who've been researching biofuels for over 30 years, are skeptical as well. According to them, ". . . severe barriers remain to ethanol from lignocellulose. The barriers look as daunting as they did 30 years ago."

Benemann says the EROEI [energy returned on energy invested] can be easily determined to be about five times as much energy required to make cellulosic ethanol than the energy contained in the ethanol.

The success of cellulosic ethanol depends on finding or engineering organisms that can tolerate extremely high concentrations of ethanol. Augenstein argues that this creature would already exist if it were possible. Organisms have had a billion years of optimization through evolution to develop a tolerance to high ethanol levels. Someone making beer, wine, or moonshine would have already discovered this creature if it could exist.

The range of chemical and physical properties in biomass, even just corn stover [leaves and stalks], is a challenge. It's hard to make cellulosic ethanol plants optimally efficient, because processes can't be tuned to such wide feedstock variation.

Where Will the Billion Tons of Biomass for Cellulosic Fuels Come From?

The government believes there is a billion tons of biomass "waste" to make cellulosic biofuels, chemicals, and generate electricity with.

The United States lost 52 million acres of cropland between 1982 and 2002. At that rate, all of the cropland will be gone in 140 years.

There isn't enough biomass to replace 30% of our petroleum use. The potential biomass energy is minuscule compared to the fossil fuel energy we consume every year. . . .

Over 25% of the "waste" biomass is expected to come from 280 million tons of corn stover. Stover is what's left after the corn grain is harvested. Another 120 million tons will come from soy and cereal straw.

There isn't enough no-till corn stover to harvest. The success of biofuels depends on corn residues. About 80% of farmers disk corn stover into the land after harvest. That renders it useless—the crop residue is buried in mud and decomposing rapidly.

Only the 20% of farmers who farm no-till will have stover to sell. The DOE Billion Ton vision assumes all farmers are no-till, 75% of residues will be harvested, and fantasizes corn and wheat yields 50% higher than now are reached.

Many tons will never be available because farmers won't sell any, or much of their residue (certainly not 75%). Many more tons will be lost due to drought, rain, or loss in storage. . . .

Farmers Aren't Stupid: They Won't Sell Their Residues

Farmers are some of the smartest people on earth or they'd soon go out of business. They have to know everything from soil science to commodity futures.

Crop production is reduced when residues are removed from the soil. Why would farmers want to sell their residues?

Harvesting of stover on the scale needed to fuel a cellulosic industry won't happen because farmers aren't stupid, especially the ones who work their own land. Although there is a wide range of opinion about the amount of residue that can be harvested safely without causing erosion, loss of soil nutrition, and soil structure, many farmers will want to be on the safe side, and stick with the studies showing that 20% to 30% at most can be harvested, not the 75% agribusiness claims is possible. Farmers also care about water quality. And farmers will decide that permanent soil compression is not worth any price. As prices of fertilizer inexorably rise due to natural gas depletion, it will be cheaper to return residues to the soil than to buy fertilizer.

Residues are a headache. The further the farmer is from the biorefinery or railroad, the slimmer the profit, and the less likely a farmer will want the extra headache and cost of hiring and scheduling many different harvesting, collection, baling, and transportation contractors for corn stover.

Residues are used by other industries. Farm managers working for distant owners are more likely to sell crop residues since they're paid to generate profits, not preserve land. But even they will sell to the highest bidder, which might be the livestock or dairy industries, furfural [industrial chemicals] factories, hydromulching companies, biocomposite manufacturers, pulp mills, or city dwellers faced with skyrocketing utility bills, since the high heating value of residue has twice the energy of the converted ethanol.

Investors aren't stupid either. If farmers can't supply enough crop residues to fuel the large biorefinery in their region, who will put up the capital to build one?

Can the Biomass Be Harvested, Baled, Stored, and Transported Economically?

Sixteen ton tractors harvest corn and spit out stover. Many of these harvesters are contracted and will continue to collect corn in the limited harvest time, not stover. If tractors are still available, the land isn't wet, snow doesn't fall, and the stover is dry, three additional tractor runs will mow, rake, and bale the stover. This will triple the compaction damage to the soil, create more erosion-prone tire tracks, increase CO_2 [carbon dioxide] emissions, add to labor costs, and put unwanted foreign matter into the bale (soil, rocks, baling wire, etc).

So biomass roadmaps call for a new type of tractor or attachment to harvest both corn and stover in one pass. But then the tractor would need to be much larger and heavier, which could cause decades-long or even permanent soil compaction. Farmers worry that mixing corn and stover might harm the quality of the grain. And on the cusp of energy descent, is it a good idea to build an even larger and more complex machine?

If the stover is harvested, the soil is now vulnerable to erosion if it rains, because there's no vegetation to protect the soil from the impact of falling raindrops. Rain also compacts the surface of the soil so that less water can enter, forcing more to run off, increasing erosion. Water landing on dense vegetation soaks into the soil, increasing plant growth and recharging underground aquifers. The more stover left on the land, the better.

The current technology to harvest residues is to put them into bales of hay. Hay is a dangerous commodity—it can spontaneously combust, and once on fire, can't be extinguished, leading to fire loss and increased fire insurance costs. Somehow the bales have to be kept from combusting during the several months it takes to dry them from 50 to 15% moisture. A large, well drained, covered area is needed to vent fumes and dissipate heat. . . .

Stover needs to be stored with a moisture content of 15% or less, but it's typically 35–50%, and rain or snow during harvest will raise these levels even higher. . . .

Residues could be stored wet, as they are in ensilage, but a great deal of R&D [research and development] are needed and to see if there are disease, pest, emission, runoff, groundwater contamination, dust, mold, or odor control problems. The amount of water required is unknown. The transit time must be short, or aerobic microbial activity will damage it. At the storage site, the wet biomass must be immediately washed, shredded, and transported to a drainage pad under a roof for storage, instead of baled when drier and left at the farm. The wet residues are heavy, making transportation costlier than for dry residues, perhaps uneconomical. It can freeze in the winter making it hard to handle. If the moisture is too low, air gets in, making aerobic fermentation possible, resulting in molds and spoilage.

Although a 6,000 dry ton per day biorefinery would have 33% lower costs than a 2,000 ton factory, the price of gas and diesel limits the distance the biofuel refinery can be from farms, since the bales are large in volume but low in density, which limits how many bales can be loaded onto a truck and transported economically.

So the "economy of scale" achieved by a very large refinery has to be reduced to a 2,000 dry ton per day biorefinery. Even this smaller refinery would require 200 trucks per hour delivering biomass during harvest season (7 × 24), or 100 trucks per day if satellite sites for storage are used. This plant would need 90% of the no-till crop residues from the surrounding 7,000 square miles with half the farmers participating. Yet less than 20% of farmers practice no-till corn and not all of the farmland is planted in corn. When this biomass is delivered to the biorefinery, it will take up at least 100 acres of land stacked 25 feet high. . . .

Too Many Barriers to Overcome

There are over 60 barriers to be overcome in making cellulosic ethanol in. . .the DOE "Roadmap for Agriculture Biomass Feedstock Supply in the United States." For example:

> *Enzyme Biochemistry.* Enzymes that exhibit high thermostability and substantial resistance to sugar end-product inhibition will be essential to fully realize enzyme-based sugar platform technology. The ability to develop such enzymes and consequently very low cost enzymatic hydrolysis technology requires increasing our understanding of the fundamental mechanisms underlying the biochemistry of enzymatic cellulose hydrolysis, including the impact of biomass structure on enzymatic cellulose decrystallization. Additional efforts aimed at understanding the role of cellulases and their interaction not only with cellulose but also the process environment is needed to affect further reductions in cellulase cost through improved production.

No wonder many of the issues with cellulosic ethanol aren't discussed—there's no way to express the problems in a sound bite.

It may not be possible to reduce the complex cellulose digesting strategies of bacteria and fungi into microorganisms or enzymes that can convert cellulose into ethanol in giant steel vats, especially given the huge physical and chemical variations in feedstock. The field of metagenomics is trying to create a chimera [new life form] from snips of genetic material of cellulose-digesting bacteria and fungi. That would be the ultimate Swiss Army-knife microbe, able to convert cellulose to sugar and then sugar to ethanol.

There's also research to replicate termite gut cellulose breakdown. Termites depend on fascinating creatures called protists in their guts to digest wood. The protists in turn outsource the work to multiple kinds of bacteria living inside of them. This is done with energy (ATP [adenosine triphosphate]) and architecture (membranes) in a system that evolved over millions of years. If the termite could fire the protists and work directly with the bacteria, that probably would have happened 50 million years ago. This process involves many kinds of bacteria, waste products, and other complexities that may not be reducible to an enzyme or a bacteria.

Finally, ethanol must be delivered. A motivation to develop cellulosic ethanol is the high delivery cost of corn grain ethanol from the Midwest to the coasts, since ethanol can't be delivered cheaply through pipelines, but must be transported by truck, rail, or barge.

The whole cellulosic ethanol enterprise falls apart if the energy returned is less than the energy invested or even one of the major stumbling blocks can't be overcome. If there isn't enough biomass, if the residues can't be stored without exploding or composting, if the oil to transport low-density residues to biorefineries or deliver the final product is too great, if no cheap enzymes or microbes are found to break down lignocellulose in wildly varying feedstocks, if the energy to clean up toxic byproducts is too expensive, or if organisms capable of tolerating high ethanol concentrations aren't found, if the barriers. . .can't be overcome, then cellulosic fuels are not going to happen.

> "We need to make sure that in trying to solve one problem—our dependence on imported oil—we do not create a far more serious one: chaos in the world food economy."

Producing Ethanol from Corn Will Hurt Food Supplies

Lester R. Brown

In the following viewpoint, Lester R. Brown calls for a moratorium on the construction of new corn ethanol processing plants. Brown says that there just isn't enough grain to supply the world with food and to fuel U.S. automobiles. If corn-guzzling fuel-ethanol facilities continue to be constructed in the United States, Brown predicts, there will be a crisis in the world food supply, especially in developing countries in Africa, Asia, and Latin America. Lester R. Brown is the president of the Earth Policy Institute, a nonprofit organization working for an environmentally sustainable economy.

As you read, consider the following questions:

1. Why is Iowa economist Robert Wisner concerned about the future of ethanol production in his state?

Lester R. Brown, "Distillery Demand for Grain to Fuel Cars Vastly Understated," Earth Policy Institute. January 4, 2007. www.earth-policy.org. Copyright © 2007 Earth Policy Institute. Reproduced by permission.

2. According to Brown, if the entire U.S. grain harvest were converted into ethanol, what percent of U.S. auto fuel needs would be met?

3. Brown suggests that the equivalent of the 2 percent of fuel supplies now coming from ethanol could be supplied several times over by doing what?

Unprecedented diversion of the world's leading grain crop to the production of fuel will affect food prices everywhere. As the world corn price rises, so too do those of wheat and rice, both because of consumer substitution among grains and because the crops compete for land. Both corn and wheat futures were already trading at 10-year highs in late 2006.

U.S. Corn Is Staple of World Food Economy

The U.S. corn crop, accounting for 40 percent of the global harvest and supplying 70 percent of the world's corn exports, looms large in the world food economy. Annual U.S. corn exports of some 55 million tons account for nearly one fourth of world grain exports. The corn harvest of Iowa alone, which edges out Illinois as the leading producer, exceeds the entire grain harvest of Canada. Substantially reducing this export flow would send shock waves throughout the world economy.

Robert Wisner, Iowa State University economist, reports that Iowa's demand for corn from processing plants that were on line, expanding, under construction, or being planned as of late 2006 totaled 2.7 billion bushels. Yet even in a good year the state harvests only 2.2 billion bushels. As distilleries compete with feeders for grain, Iowa could become a corn importer.

Tightening Corn Supplies

With corn supplies tightening fast, rising prices will affect not only products made directly from corn, such as breakfast cereals, but also those produced using corn, including milk, eggs, cheese, butter, poultry, pork, beef, yogurt, and ice cream. The risk is that soaring food prices could generate a consumer backlash against the fuel ethanol industry.

Fuel ethanol proponents point out, and rightly so, that the use of corn to produce ethanol is not a total loss to the food economy because 30 percent of the corn is recovered in distillers dried grains that can be fed to beef and dairy cattle, pigs, and chickens, though only in limited amounts. They also argue that the U.S. distillery demand for corn can be met by expanding land in corn, mostly at the expense of soybeans, and by raising yields. While it is true that the corn crop can be expanded, there is no precedent for growth on the scale needed. And this soaring demand for corn comes when world grain production has fallen below consumption in six of the last seven years, dropping grain stocks to their lowest level in 34 years.

Food vs. Fuel

From an agricultural vantage point, the automotive demand for fuel is insatiable. The grain it takes to fill a 25-gallon tank with ethanol just once will feed one person for a whole year. Converting the entire U.S. grain harvest to ethanol would satisfy only 16 percent of U.S. auto fuel needs.

The competition for grain between the world's 800 million motorists who want to maintain their mobility and its 2 billion poorest people who are simply trying to survive is emerging as an epic issue. Soaring food prices could lead to urban food riots in scores of lower-income countries that rely on grain imports, such as Indonesia, Egypt, Algeria, Nigeria, and Mexico. The resulting political instability could in turn disrupt global economic progress, directly affecting all countries. It is not only food prices that are at stake, but trends in the Nikkei [Japanese stock market] Index and the [U.S. stock market] Dow Jones Industrials as well.

High Food, Fuel Prices Hurt Poor the Most

Hunger, said [economist and philosopher] Amartya Sen, results not from scarcity, but poverty. According to the FAO [United Nations Food and Agriculture Organization], there is enough food in the world to supply everyone with a daily 3,500-calorie diet of fresh fruit, nuts, vegetables, dairy and meat. Nonetheless, because they are poor, 824 million people continue to go hungry. In 2000, world leaders promised to halve the proportion of hungry people living in extreme poverty by 2015. Little progress has been made. The world's poorest people already spend 50–80% of their total household income on food. They suffer when high fuel prices push up food prices. Now, because food and fuel crops are competing for land and resources, high food prices may actually push up fuel prices. Both increase the price of land and water. This perverse, inflationary spiral puts food and productive resources out of reach for the poor. The International Food Policy Research Institute warns that the price of basic food staples could increase 20–33% by the year 2010 and 26–135% by the year 2020. Caloric consumption typically declines as price rises by a ratio of 1:2. With every one percent rise in the cost of food, 16 million people are made food insecure. If current trends continue, some 1.2 billion people could be chronically hungry by 2025—600 million more than previously predicted. World food aid will not likely come to the rescue because surpluses will go into our gas tanks. What are urgently needed are massive transfers of food-producing resources to the rural poor; not converting land to fuel production.

Eric Holt-Giménez,
"BioFuels: Myths of the Agro-fuels Transitions,"
Institute for Food and Development Policy,
July 6, 2007. www.foodfirst.org.

Alternatives to Corn Ethanol

There are alternatives to creating a crop-based automotive fuel economy. The equivalent of the 2 percent of U.S. automotive fuel supplies now coming from ethanol could be achieved several times over, and at a fraction of the cost, by raising auto fuel efficiency standards by 20 percent.

If we shift to gas-electric hybrid plug-in cars over the next decade, we could be doing short-distance driving, such as the daily commute or grocery shopping, with electricity. If we then invested in thousands of wind farms to feed cheap electricity into the grid, U.S. cars could run primarily on wind energy—and at the gasoline equivalent of less than $1 a gallon. The stage is set for a crash program to help Detroit switch to gas-electric hybrid plug-in cars.

Ethanol Plant Moratorium Is Needed

It is time for a moratorium on the licensing of new distilleries, a time-out, while we catch our breath and decide how much corn can be used for ethanol without dramatically raising food prices. The policy goal should be to use just enough fuel ethanol to support corn prices and farm incomes but not so much that it disrupts the world food economy. Meanwhile, a much greater effort is needed to produce ethanol from cellulosic sources such as switchgrass, a feedstock that is not used for food.

The world desperately needs a strategy to deal with the emerging food-fuel battle. As the leading grain producer, grain exporter, and ethanol producer, the United States is in the driver's seat. We need to make sure that in trying to solve one problem—our dependence on imported oil—we do not create a far more serious one: chaos in the world food economy.

VIEWPOINT 6

| "A lot of [the] fuel-versus-feed argu-
| ments do not stack up."

Producing Ethanol from Corn Will Not Hurt Food Supplies

Patrick Mazza

In the following viewpoint, Patrick Mazza argues that the emergence of corn ethanol as an automotive fuel is exposing a flawed U.S. agricultural policy that sends cheap corn from the United States overseas and discourages farmers in developing countries from producing their own crops. Reporting on the 2007 "Business of Biofuels" conference in Gresham, Oregon, Mazza draws the conclusion that the fuel-versus-food debate is exaggerated, and that higher corn prices may actually be good for farmers in the developing world, as it will make their locally grown crops more valuable. Patrick Mazza is research director for Climate Solutions, a nonprofit organization dedicated to finding solutions to global warming.

As you read, consider the following questions:

1. According to Brent Searle of the Oregon Department of Agriculture, how much does corn sweetener add to the cost of a can of soda?

Patrick Mazza, "Growing Sustainable Biofuels: The Sustainability Opportunity," *Harvesting Clean Energy Journal*, October 2, 2007. Reproduced by permission.

2. According to Mazza, what caused corn exports to Mexico to increase 240 percent?

3. According to a *Wall Street Journal* report, how much money did the United States spend shipping commodities to Ethiopia in 2003? How much did the United States spend on agricultural development in Ethiopia?

The biofuels boom has brought on a backlash, and the biofuels community is beginning to mount a response. This was in evidence at the second annual Business of Biofuels Conference in Gresham, Oregon in September [2007]. One of its two days was devoted to sustainability issues, particularly the interaction of food and fuel crops.

Keynoter Jim Kleinschmidt of the Institute for Agriculture and Trade Policy [IATP] mapped the landscape.

Biofuels Issue Reveals Weaknesses in U.S. Policy

"Today there is no question, biofuels are becoming mainstream, a real part of today's agriculture, energy and forestry agenda," said the IATP Rural Communities Program director. "But there are consequences," noting food security concerns are one of the greatest. "The backlash against biofuels is growing. We are now at risk of losing the public support needed for expansion of biofuels markets."

Kleinschmidt said biofuels growth is underscoring and amplifying problems created by existing agricultural policies. That opens the way for biofuels to promote sustainable agricultural policies. . . .

A significant problem with the current system is policies that promote only a few major commodities. This was cited by speakers throughout the day, including Brent Searle of the Oregon Department of Agriculture. Searle noted the natural tendency of farmers is toward producing the largest crop they can with available land and equipment. Commodity support programs have reinforced this tendency. So sectors ranging from livestock to ethanol have been built on an assumption of grain supplies below the cost of production. Now changing markets are having ripple effects across sectors. Livestock operators in particular have seen their costs go up.

Fuel-Versus-Feed Argument Does Not Stack Up

Ethanol industry demand for corn is "no doubt" having an impact, Kleinschmidt said. However, inflation-adjusted prices are well below 1970s levels and "merely returning to levels that let farmers make a living." (Indeed, corn subsidies will decline 75 percent [in 2007], reducing program costs by $6 billion.)

Yet the impact of corn prices on overall food costs has been exaggerated, Searle said. He quoted American Farm Bureau Federation Senior Economist Terry Francl, ". . .there is little evidence that any food category has been affected by higher corn prices in any significant manner. Certainly it is true that some food product manufacturers have claimed higher corn prices are increasing their manufacturing cost, using this as a justification for raising their product prices."

As evidence Searle noted that even at $4 per bushel,

- a 10-ounce box of corn flakes contains less than a nickel's worth or corn,

- corn sweetener in a can of soda adds two cents to the cost,

- corn feed represents 25 cents at retail for pork at $3 a pound.

"It's important to look at the big picture," Searle said. "A lot of these fuel-versus-feed arguments do not stack up. Ethanol from corn is transitory," Searle said. "My concern is we don't kill the good to try to achieve the perfect."

Price of Corn Not Only Reason Food Costs More

Current fluctuations in food prices from increased demand for corn for ethanol do not represent a permanent competition between fuel demand and food security.

Food prices increased 4.1 percent in the United States from June 2006 to June 2007 due not only to increased corn prices, but also increased costs of oil, worldwide weather-related disruptions of food (droughts and freezes), and contamination scares. The costs of all goods, excluding energy and food, rose 2.2 percent in the same period, according to the U.S. Department of Labor, Bureau of Labor Statistics (BLS), which compiles the Consumer Price Index.

According to BLS, rising energy prices accounted for 48 percent of the overall rise in the Consumer Price Index, while food prices accounted for 17 percent.

According to Iowa State University's Center for Agricultural and Rural Development (CARD), traders have anticipated higher prices and have built them into futures contracts. Most of the anticipated price changes have already shown up in market prices.

Further, higher corn and crop prices increase income for farmers throughout the world. According to the United Nations Energy report *Sustainable Bioenergy: A Framework for Decision Makers*, "As biofuels absorb crop surpluses in industrialized countries, commodity prices will rise, increasing income for farmers in poor countries."

"Myths and Facts: Food and Fuel,"
Biotechnology Industry Organization,
June 20, 2007. www.bio.org.

Cellulose Can Supply Ethanol of Future

The next stage of biofuels is a move from grain to cellulose feedstocks. This is one opportunity for the biofuels sector to promote overall agricultural sustainability. Kleinschmidt called for support for a greater diversity of crops, in particular perennial grasses that can feed cellulosic biofuels production. In addition, "Biofuels need to embrace the local." An emphasis on regional biofuels feedstocks will go hand in hand with an emphasis on local food production. In the U.S. this task may fall to the states, he noted.

"The biofuels sector needs to promote all forms of renewable energy," Kleinschmidt added, including electricity for plug-in hybrids and renewables at biofuels plants.

Representing the largest ethanol producer in the western U.S., Tim Raphael of Pacific Ethanol said, "Corn ethanol producers are leading a lot of the work on next generation cellulosic ethanol." That includes companies such as Broin, planning to add cellulosic production to a standard corn plant, and his own. Pacific is seeking funding to use straw and wood waste at its Boardman, Oregon plant and plans to eventually use cellulose at all its plants.

Use of cellulose will take pressure off food crops while reducing global warming emissions more than corn ethanol. But corn is needed for the transition, Raphael said.

"We can't get there from here without access to markets today. Corn ethanol producers are going to play a key role in bringing on the next generation."

Higher U.S. Corn Prices Help Farmers in Developing Countries

The impact of biofuels growth on developing nations' food supplies has drawn some of the sharpest backlashing along the lines of "starving the poor to feed our cars." Speakers during the day focused on the larger context, another one of those ways the biofuels boom is amplifying the effects of poor policy choices. Kleinschmidt pointed to trade policies that promote dumping below-cost commodities to foreign markets, particularly in developing countries. He noted that corn exports to Mexico have increased 240 percent since the North American Free Trade Agreement [NAFTA] went into effect in 1994. So when tortilla prices escalate, biofuels receive the blame.

It should be remembered that when NAFTA went into effect, and the Zapatista army appeared in Chiapas, Mexico in protest, the coming invasion by subsidized corn was a major driver. Indigenous Mayans, probably the world's original corn farmers, were worried they would be driven out of business. And their fears were well founded. Hundreds of thousands of poor Mexican farmers have been driven off the land, and pressure on U.S. borders has intensified as a result.

Kleinschmidt called for an end to trade policies that dump commodities on developing nations. Instead, higher prices and positive policies can improve the lot of farmers in those nations.

Raphael echoed that comment. U.S. food aid programs "should be investing in local agriculture, not relying on cheap U.S. commodities." He quoted a *Wall Street Journal* report that showed the U.S. in 2003 spent $500 million shipping commodities to Ethiopia while spending only $5 million on agricultural development there. He cited a quote from Charles Uphaus of Bread for the World, "If the U.S. is serious about addressing world hunger, the way to do that is increasing production, not shipping U.S. commodities. . .around the world."

Raphael also quoted Suzanne Hunt of Worldwatch Institute: "If rich countries were no longer dumping cheap food on the commodities market, farmers in developing nations would have a better chance of staying in business."

Biofuels growth has placed new stresses and pressures on agriculture, underscoring the need for sustainability in production of all commodities whether they are food, feed, fiber or fuel. Biofuels represent an opportunity to put in place the policies that will achieve a more sustainable agricultural system overall in the U.S. and around the world.

Periodical Bibliography

The following articles have been selected to supplement the diverse views presented in this chapter.

Kevin Bullis — "Ethanol from Garbage and Old Tires: A Versatile New Process for Making Biofuels Could Slash Their Cost," *Technology Review.* March–April 2008.

Tom Carney — "The Ethanol Option: 'Quick, Easy Route' to Combating Energy Crisis Is Not Sustainable, Many Say," *National Catholic Reporter.* October 26, 2007.

Jim Giles — "Biofuels Emissions May Be 'Worse Than Petrol,'" *New Scientist.* February 2008.

Diane Greer — "Realities, Opportunities for Cellulosic Ethanol," *BioCycle.* January 2007.

Steve Hargreaves — "Debunking the Ethanol Bust," *CNNMoney.com.* October 2, 2007.

Glenn Hess — "Renewable Fuels Face Bumpy Road," *Chemical & Engineering News.* September 17, 2007.

Spencer Hunt — "Ethanol: Is Corn-Based Fuel Worth Tax Deals, Pollution?" *The Columbus Dispatch.* August 6, 2007.

Byron King — "Why Ethanol Cannot Live Up to All the 'Perfect' Energy-Solution Hype," *Whiskey & Gunpowder Special Report.* 2007.

Clifford Krauss — "Ethanol's Boom Stalling as Glut Depresses Price," *New York Times.* September 30, 2007.

Stan Levine — "The End of Big Oil," *The New Republic.* February 27, 2008.

Ian Lewis — "Sunny Days Ahead," *Petroleum Economist.* August 2007.

OPPOSING
VIEWPOINTS®
SERIES

CHAPTER 4

How Should the Government Promote Renewable Energy and Fuels?

Chapter Preface

It takes about 20 million barrels each day to satisfy America's thirst for oil, and over half of this amount is imported from other countries. Most of the world's oil reserves are in volatile regions of the world and oil prices are increasing rapidly. In early 2008, the price of oil hit $100 per barrel. Most Americans agree that the country needs to reduce its consumption of foreign oil. Some people believe that this can be achieved by drilling for oil in the Arctic National Wildlife Refuge (ANWR). However, other people believe that the oil that would be obtained by opening up ANWR to drilling isn't worth the harm it would cause to Alaskan wildlife.

ANWR is a vast expanse of government-protected land located in the northeast corner of Alaska, north of the Arctic Circle and south of the North Pole. In the 1950s, naturalists Olaus and Margaret Murie visited this then-unnamed area and noted large numbers of migrating caribou. They and other conservation groups began a campaign to protect the area's caribou and other wildlife. In 1960, one year after Alaska was formally recognized as a state, the Arctic National Wildlife Refuge was established under an order of the U.S. Secretary of the Interior. The original size of ANWR was about 8 million acres.

In 1980, the U.S. Congress enacted the Alaska National Interest Lands Conservation Act (ANILCA). Under this act, ANWR expanded to include an additional 9.2 million acres. ANILCA designated much of the original 8 million acres as a wilderness area. However, one part of the original range, the coastal plain, was not included as a wilderness area. Congress wanted more information about the coastal plain. Under section 1002 of ANILCA, the government was directed to study the fish and wildlife, as well as the oil resources, in the coastal plain.

The U.S. government released the "Section 1002 Report" in 1987. The report said that the coastal plain contained outstanding petroleum reserves and it recommended that the United States develop the oil in the region. However, the report also found that the section 1002 area was the most biologically productive part of the entire Arctic Refuge, and that developing the oil resources in the coastal plain could adversely impact caribou, polar and grizzly bears, and nesting birds.

As of March 2008, the petroleum reserves in ANWR remain untapped. However, the question of whether or not to drill for oil in the coastal plain has been debated almost continuously since the 1970s. Each time the country faces energy challenges the debate intensifies. Traditionally, Alaskan trade unions, business interests, and some non-Native residents have supported drilling in the refuge, while environmental groups have opposed it. Among Native Alaskan tribes, support is mixed.

Those who oppose drilling in ANWR say that the region represents one of the only undisturbed arctic habitats in the world. According to the Wilderness Society, ANWR is home to more than 250 animal species, including wolves, grizzlies, caribou, and millions of migrating birds. ANWR is often called America's Serengeti because, like the famous African savannah, it provides habitat to an enormous number of species in a unique and ancient ecosystem.

Drilling in the coastal plain would be particularly harmful, says Greenpeace, an environmental activist group. The coastal plain is the preferred area where caribou go to give birth to their calves in the spring. Studies show that pregnant caribou are extremely sensitive to disruptions in the environment. The Wilderness Society concurs.

The Natural Resources Defense Council (NRDC) says "there may be no more than 3.2 billion barrels of economically recoverable oil in the coastal plain of ANWR, a drop in the bucket that would do virtually nothing to ease America's energy problems." The NRDC further claims that ANWR's total output would amount to "no more than a six-month supply of oil for the United States—far too little to have a long-term impact on prices. And consumers could wait up to a decade to reap any benefits, because drilling could begin only after much wrangling over leases, environmental permits and regulatory review."

Those who support ANWR drilling disagree about the area's oil potential. They say that the oil in ANWR could significantly reduce oil imports and increase the nation's energy security. Oil industry estimates say that ANWR could contain more than 10 billion barrels of oil—twice the proven reserves of Texas and an amount equivalent to roughly 30 years' worth of Saudi Arabian oil imports. Replacing oil imports with oil from ANWR could save the country hundreds of billions of dollars, and make the United States less dependent on unstable regions of the world.

Supporters of drilling say that oil development and wildlife conservation can coexist in ANWR. ANWR Power, a pro-drilling organization, says, "the Coastal Plain is no Serengeti. It is a vast desert of frozen tundra, without trees or mountains." Furthermore, ANWR Power claims that the wildlife that does live or travel through the plain won't be harmed by oil drilling. Oil drilling would only take place on 2,000 acres within the coastal plain, an area smaller than Disney World. In recent years, advanced technologies have dramatically reduced the environmental footprint of oil drilling and minimized impacts to surrounding wildlife. Proponents of drilling point out that the central Arctic caribou herd that lives near America's prolific Prudhoe Bay oil fields has grown 1,000 percent since oil development began in that region.

Should the U.S. Congress and the president open ANWR for oil and gas development in order to respond to rising oil imports, or should the area's unique ecosystem be given permanent protection from development? This is just one of many questions the U.S. government is wrangling with in trying to solve the many energy challenges facing the nation. Congress is also debating whether or not to promote renewable energy, and if so, how. In the following chapter, the contributors provide their viewpoints on the merits of certain renewable energy policies.

> *"The expanded use of renewable and alternative fuels supports [President George W. Bush's] goals of enhanced energy security and strengthened environmental protection."*

A National Renewable Fuels Standard Is Beneficial

Robert Meyers

In the following viewpoint, Robert Meyers testifies before the U.S. House of Representatives Subcommittee on Energy and Air Quality on the issue of renewable energy. He argues that expanding the use of renewable and alternative fuels can reduce the country's dependence on foreign oil and reduce greenhouse gas emissions. Meyers explains the merits of the Renewable Fuel Standard (RFS), enacted by Congress in 2005 to increase transportation fuels in the nation's fuel supply, and claims that not only is the RFS beneficial, but it should be expanded to include alternative fuels, as called for in the "Twenty in Ten" plan. Robert Meyers works for the Office of Air and Radiation of the U.S. Environmental Protection Agency.

Robert Meyers, "Testimony Before the U.S. House of Representatives Committee on Energy and Commerce Subcommittee on Energy and Air Quality," May 8, 2007.

As you read, consider the following questions:

1. According to Meyers, what is the difference between the Alternative Fuels Standard and the Renewable Fuels Standard?

2. What is the National RFS Rule and what should it accomplish, according to Meyers?

3. What will a transition to renewable fuels do to auto emissions, according to the Environmental Protection Agency?

M r. Chairman, and members of the Subcommittee, I appreciate the opportunity to come before you today to testify on how the expanded use of renewable and alternative fuels supports [President George W. Bush's] goals of enhanced energy security and strengthened environmental protection.

The "Twenty in Ten" Plan

In his 2007 State of the Union Address, the President challenged the nation to address our growing reliance on oil. He called for reducing gasoline consumption by 20 percent in the next 10 years, while doing so in a way that keeps America's economy growing and protects our environment. This "Twenty in Ten" plan includes a proposed requirement for 35 billion gallons of alternative fuel in 2017. This aggressive goal would build upon EPA's [U.S. Environmental Protection Agency] current Renewable Fuel Standard, or RFS program, and require the use of renewable and alternative fuel well beyond the 2012 target set by the Energy Policy Act of 2005 (EPAct 2005). Expanding this mandate is expected to decrease projected gasoline use by 15 percent. The President's plan seeks to achieve another five percent reduction in gasoline consumption through the Administration's proposal to reform CAFE [Corporate Average Fuel Economy] standards for passenger cars and to extend the current light truck rule. The President's energy plans also emphasize the energy security benefits of increasing domestic oil and gas production and doubling the current capacity of the Strategic Petroleum Reserve [the largest emergency petroleum reserve in the world].

"Twenty in Ten" would diversify the sources and types of fuels we use, while reducing our vulnerability to supply disruptions, sudden price increases, and our overall dependence on oil. At the same time, the plan could help confront the serious challenge of climate change. Attaining these goals will require significant advancements in technology and careful assessment of their benefits and costs. Most importantly, Congress must pass legislation to allow these programs to become a reality.

The Alternative Fuels Standard Builds upon the Renewable Fuels Standard

The Administration's proposed Alternative Fuels Standard [AFS] sets forth an ambitious, but achievable, path forward for an expansion of the use of renewable and alternative fuels. The AFS specifies that 35 billion gallons of alternative fuel be used in the nation's transportation fuel by the year 2017. The AFS would include all fuels that are currently part of the RFS and would include fuels currently classified as "alternative fuels" under the Energy Policy Act. It would also allow other types of fuels to qualify as alternatives for compliance, adding competition in the alternative fuel marketplace. The AFS includes fuels or fuel components such as ethanol (derived from a variety of sources, including corn and cellulosic feedstock), biodiesel, butanol, as well as other alternatives to crude oil-based fuels such as natural gas, hydrogen, and coal-to-liquids. The AFS would also include the use of electricity to power advanced vehicles, including "plug-in" hybrid vehicles. . . .

On April 10, [2007] [EPA administrator Stephen] Johnson signed the National Renewable Fuels Standard Rule, which establishes a comprehensive program that will lead to more than doubling the amount of renewable fuel use between 2006

Americans Support Renewable Fuels Standard

Americans of all stripes agree: We want greater use of renewable fuels like ethanol. According to a new national poll released today by the Renewable Fuels Now Coalition, 74 percent of Americans believe we should increase our use of domestically produced renewable fuels like ethanol.

In addition, 87 percent of Americans maintain the federal government should actively support the development of a renewable fuels industry in this country, and 77 percent think Congress should encourage oil refiners to blend more ethanol into their gasoline products.

"By overwhelming margins, Americans want renewable fuels like ethanol to play a larger role in our nation's energy future," said Renewable Fuels Association President Bob Dinneen, a member of the Renewable Fuels Now Coalition. "The consequences of continuing our dependence on foreign oil are unacceptable. Renewable fuels like ethanol offer our nation an opportunity to go in a new, more sustainable energy direction."

Dinneen continued, "These numbers make it clear that the American public understands the benefits of renewable fuels like ethanol and believes the federal government has a role to play in developing a robust renewable fuels industry in this country. By passing an energy bill complete with an expansion and acceleration of the Renewable Fuels Standard, Congress would mirror the desire of the American public to move away from our growing dependence on foreign—and often hostile—sources of oil."

"Nearly Three out of Four Americans Want Increased Renewable Fuel Use, Production," Renewable Fuels Now, *October 30, 2007.*

and 2012. This landmark rule provides market certainty for the expanded production and use of renewable fuels by requiring minimum amounts of renewable fuel volumes to be used in our nation's transportation fuel supply. It also establishes important compliance and implementation measures necessary to assure that these minimum volumes are met. The AFS would build upon the recently completed RFS regulation—the first milestone in increasing the amount of domestically produced renewable fuels used in motor vehicles.

The core compliance measure of the RFS, the credit trading program, was carefully designed by EPA staff in close collaboration with various stakeholders. It works with the existing markets by allowing renewable fuels to be blended when and where it makes sense, while maintaining the necessary flexibility to expand the number and types of fuels as they come to the market.

RFS Results in Reductions in Petroleum Use and Many Emissions

EPA conducted a number of detailed analyses of the RFS program, including the energy, emissions, air quality, and economic impacts of expanded renewable fuel use. These impacts vary depending on the volume and type of renewable fuel anticipated to be used. Our analyses projected fuel use in 2012 using both the minimum volume of renewable fuel required under EPAct 2005 and higher volumes projected in the Energy Information Administration's 2006 Annual Energy Outlook. Thus, the results of EPA's analysis show a range based on these two projections using a 2004 baseline.

With regard to petroleum consumption impacts, EPA estimates that this transition to renewable fuels will result in reductions of between 2.0 and 3.9 billion gallons of petroleum consumption, or roughly 0.8 to 1.6 percent of the approximately 250 billion gallons of petroleum that would otherwise be used in the transportation sector in 2012. EPA also projected that the RFS also will achieve reductions in carbon dioxide equivalent greenhouse gas emissions between 8.0 and 13.1 million metric tons, or about 0.4 to 0.6 percent of the anticipated greenhouse gas emissions from the transportation sector in the United States in 2012. EPA's analyses additionally found that with regard to other emissions impacts, this program could help reduce carbon monoxide emissions from gasoline-powered vehicles and equipment between 0.9 and 2.5 percent and emissions of benzene, a toxic mobile source air pollutant, between 1.8 and 4.0 percent.

At the same time, however, other vehicle emissions may increase, including volatile organic compounds, or VOC's, and oxides of nitrogen, or NOx, both of which are precursors of ozone. These effects will vary significantly by region: areas that already use ethanol blended into gasoline will experience little or no additional change in vehicle emissions or air quality. Those areas where ethanol use increases substantially as a result of the RFS program may see an increase in VOC emissions between 4 and 5 percent and an increase in NOx emissions between 6 and 7 percent from gasoline-powered vehicles and equipment. Emissions of certain air toxics, like acetaldehyde, also increase although the overall volume of such emissions is not large in comparison with the volume of reductions in benzene.

EPA's analysis also included a look at the potential impacts on the nation's agricultural sector. This work found that an increase in the use of renewable fuels associated with the RFS promotes rural development by increasing annual aggregate farm income between $2.7 and $5.4 billion dollars in 2012. In addition, EPA's analysis estimated a possible modest increase in food costs and a potential decrease in exports of certain agricultural commodities such as corn. . . .

AFS, RFS Needed to Reduce Dependence on Foreign Oil

Altogether, the President's AFS proposal recognizes the critical need to reduce our nation's dependence on foreign oil as well as to address rising emissions of greenhouse gases from motor vehicles and off-road vehicles. EPA's success in crafting and adopting RFS regulations under EPAct 2005 has proven to be a critical first step in the national expansion of renewable and alternative fuel use in the transportation sector. As Congress considers ways to build on this success, the country now has a model that should help assure the long-term viability of a renewable and alternative fuels program. EPA stands ready to work with Congress to enact the Alternative Fuel Standard into law.

"While the infrastructure challenges loom large, other concerns also surround the new Renewable Fuel Standard, including the environmental impacts of increased biofuels production."

Implementation and Environmental Concerns Surround the National Renewable Fuel Standard

Rosalie Westenskow

In the following viewpoint, Rosalie Westenskow says that some congressional leaders are questioning whether the Renewable Fuel Standard (RFS), is a practical solution to decreasing domestic greenhouse gas emissions and U.S. dependence on foreign oil. The Senate Committee on Energy and Natural Resources worries that portions of the law will be difficult to enact, such as the early year biofuel requirements. Environmental impacts of increased biofuels production, such as increased soil erosion, greenhouse gas emissions, and fertilizer runoff, as well as a disruption of food supply, are also concerns. Rosalie Westenskow is a United Press International *correspondent.*

As you read, consider the following questions:

1. According to Jeff Bingaman, chairman of the Senate Committee on Energy and Natural Resources, what are the three major problems with the Renewable Fuel Standard?
2. Why is it difficult and expensive to get biofuels to consumers?
3. Why could the increased demand for ethanol that will result from the Renewable Fuel Standard prolong our reliance on other countries for fuel?

Just weeks after passing a major energy bill, some congressional leaders are questioning whether certain portions of the law are achievable.

The biggest concerns hinge on the Renewable Fuel Standard [RFS] established by the Energy Independence and Security Act of 2007, a massive piece of legislation signed by the president on Dec. 19. The provision mandates increasing amounts of biofuels be produced and mixed with domestic gasoline. The dictated volume grows steadily each year, requiring a nearly eight-fold increase overall from last year's production of 4.7 billion gallons to 36 billion gallons in 2022.

While the law as a whole has the potential to significantly decrease U.S. dependence on foreign oil and domestic greenhouse gas emissions, the RFS provision could prove difficult to enact as it is currently constructed, said Sen. Jeff Bingaman, D-N.M., at a hearing Thursday in the Senate Committee on Energy and Natural Resources.

"First, early year biofuel requirements could be too aggressive; second, mandates for specific technologies and feedstock could prove to be overly prescriptive; finally, the environmental restrictions may be too narrow," said Bingaman, chairman of the committee.

The RFS requires biofuel production to almost double in 2008 alone. While Bingaman said he's confident the biofuels industry can produce the 8.5 billion mandated gallons, getting it to consumers presents a daunting task.

"It is not clear how all of this biofuel will find its way into the fuel tanks of our cars and trucks," Bingaman said. "Because the law was signed only weeks before the 2008 requirement came into effect, refiners had no opportunity to ensure that sufficient infrastructure would be in place to handle that much of an increase."

Indeed, representatives of the petrochemical and refining industries say the infrastructure needed this year alone cannot be built quickly enough.

Currently, most of the biofuels used domestically are consumed in the East Coast, West Coast, upper Midwest and Texas. But in order to meet the RFS, biofuels must be blended into gasoline sold all over the country, said Charles Drevna, president of the National Petrochemical and Refiners Association, an advocacy group for the industry.

"When you start going beyond these traditional areas, it is a very, very difficult and expensive proposition to get" biofuels to consumers, Drevna told United Press International. "The cost of transporting renewable fuels to gas stations could reach 13 cents to 18 cents per gallon."

Ethanol, the major biofuel used today, cannot be transported via pipeline, like conventional fuels, because of its corrosive properties and its ability to absorb the water commonly present in pipelines, rendering it unusable.

However, ethanol industry advocates say the infrastructure challenges are not insurmountable. The industry has established a "virtual pipeline" using the rail system, barges and trucks, said Bob Dinneen, president of the Renewable Fuels Association, a trade association for the industry.

"We can move product quickly to those areas where it is needed," Dinneen told senators Thursday.

A new ethanol distribution center in Manley, Iowa, will provide needed infrastructure, Dinneen said. By the end of

2009 more than 75 ethanol plants are expected to be operating within 275 miles of the terminal, producing about 5 billion gallons per year.

While the infrastructure challenges loom large, other concerns also surround the new RFS, including the environmental impacts of increased biofuels production.

The most commercially viable and commonly consumed biofuel today is ethanol, produced mainly, in the United States, from corn. Unfortunately, converting more land to grow these crops for ethanol could increase soil erosion, greenhouse gas emissions and fertilizer runoff, as well as disrupt food supply, according to several studies.

The increased demand for ethanol that will result from the new RFS could also potentially prolong our reliance on other countries for fuel, said Mark Muller of the Institute for Agriculture and Trade Policy, a non-profit advocacy group.

"This could lead to removing the tariff on Brazilian ethanol, resulting in a floodgate of cheap Brazilian ethanol driving down the domestic ethanol price, and thwarting U.S. efforts to become more energy independent," Muller told UPI.

That's unlikely, said Brian Jennings, executive vice president of the American Coalition for Ethanol.

"We have such a tremendous potential to produce fuel in the United States that the demand can be met domestically," he said.

Ethanol won't be the only fuel used to satisfy the RFS, though. By 2022, 21 billion of the 36 billion gallons of mandated biofuels must come from "advanced sources" produced from wastes, debris and non-food crops.

To date, significant volumes of fuel have not been produced from any "advanced sources," but they hold huge potential, according to several sources. One study, conducted by the Oregon Environmental Council, found 84 million gallons of ethanol could be produced annually from the state's wheat residues.

Renewable Fuel Standard Is Bad Policy

The new ethanol mandate is perhaps the most disappointing program in the Energy Policy Act of 2005. Since taking effect in 2006, this measure has increased energy and food prices while doing little to reduce oil imports or improve the environment.

Based on this track record, the Administration and Congress should now be debating the repeal of this ill-advised and anti-consumer measure. Instead, in his State of the Union address, President George W. Bush proposed greatly expanding the mandate. Regrettably, this may be one of the few energy policy ideas upon which he and Congress can agree.

Any effort to increase the ethanol mandate is misguided because it would exacerbate the problems created by the current requirements without appreciably reducing oil imports or protecting the environment.

Ben Lieberman
"The Ethanol Mandate Should Not Be Expanded,"
The Heritage Foundation. April 11, 2007.

However, there are concerns that key fuel sources have been excluded from the bill. The most egregious of these is woody biomass derived from federal forest lands, said Carol Werner, executive director of the Environmental and Energy Study Institute, a non-profit organization.

Forests cover one-third of U.S. land, and much of that area could be routinely thinned of debris—reducing fire hazards and providing material for fuel, Werner said.

"Unfortunately, these provisions eliminate an opportunity to support hazardous fuels reduction (and) reduce the number of possible cellulosic (sources) for production of renewable fuels," Werner told senators Thursday.

The potential amount of woody biomass excluded by the provision is no paltry figure. According to a study conducted by the Department of Energy and Oak Ridge National Laboratory in 2005, 1,996 million dry tons of forest biomass could be gleaned by thinning areas with a high fire risk in national forests alone.

Although the law technically allows biomass from high fire risk areas to count toward the RFS, "high fire risk" is defined as "being next to an occupied building," effectively eliminating most federal forest land, said Matt Letourneau, Republican communications director for the Senate Energy Committee.

Although no plans have been formally made to alter the law, Congress could potentially pass a corrections bill to iron out some of the difficulties in implementing the RFS, Letourneau said.

"There's been talk of making some technical corrections anyway," he told UPI. "(And) there are also potential opportunities to attach language to other legislation."

Whatever Congress decides to do, it's clear implementation will be a challenge, said Sen. Pete Domenici, R-N.M.

"I think it is pretty obvious that either a lot of good administrative people will have to get together and resolve this in a way that would be extraordinary or we'll have to end up changing things," Domenici said.

> "A national renewable portfolio stan-
> dard is the most direct policy option for
> Congress to. . .fulfill their responsibility
> to ensure affordable, reliable, secure,
> and clean sources of energy for the
> American public."

A National Renewable Portfolio Standard Is Beneficial

Jaime Steve

*In the following viewpoint, Jaime Steve argues that a federal "re-
newable portfolio standard," or RPS, would provide myriad national benefits and alleviate many of the country's energy problems. Under a federal RPS, renewable energy sources, such as
wind and solar, would make up a required amount of electric
utility production. A federal RPS would help address global
warming, increase energy security, and stimulate the economy,
according to Steve. Jaime Steve is the director of legislative affairs
of the American Wind Energy Association.*

Jaime Steve, "Letter to U.S. Representative John D. Dingell, Chairman, House Committee on Energy and Commerce, and Rick Boucher, Chairman, Subcommittee on Energy
and Air Quality," American Wind Energy Association, June 22, 2007. Reproduced by
permission.

As you read, consider the following questions:

1. According to Steve, what was the purpose of the Energy Policy Act of 2005?
2. According to a report released by the consulting group Wood Mackenzie, what would be the impact of a 15 percent national renewable portfolio standard?
3. What does the author think would happen to the demand for natural gas under a national renewable portfolio standard?

Not only is adopting a federal "renewable portfolio standard" advisable, it is a prudent, beneficial and necessary policy that the nation can pursue in order to address global warming, energy security, rural economic development and manufacturing jobs.

A Federal RPS Is Critical and Timely

The U.S. electricity sector faces serious challenges in finding deployable carbon-free sources. Renewable energy, particularly wind energy, along with energy efficiency, are the only technologies that are currently available, vastly deployable, and cost-effective that can address these issues today, and can do so at a cost savings while bringing additional benefits to the American public.

The issues that we face today, making portfolio standards one of the most critical and advisable policies for Congress, include:

- national security stemming from importing fossil fuels, which now includes coal and an increasing amount of natural gas, along with petroleum, from unstable nations,

- fuel price volatility faced by electric utilities and consumers due to demand and supply imbalances in the domestic and international fossil fuel and energy markets,

- decreased electric reliability from a constrained transmission system and lack of investment in generation build out to keep up with increasing electricity demand,

- impacts on human and environmental health from conventional pollutants and increasingly stringent regulations to address these impacts,

- threat of greenhouse gas emission impacts on global climate and ecosystems, potential for regulations, risk from regulatory uncertainty, and

- impending cost associated with addressing all of these issues.

The timeliness of pursuing a policy that creates a market for renewable energy to become a significant source of electric generation will not only address all of the issues above in a cost-effective manner, but will bring additional benefits of:

- restoring U.S. leadership in renewable energy production,

- creating hundreds of thousands of jobs in manufacturing and construction sectors,

- building domestic manufacturing facilities to keep pace with increasing production of renewable energy generating capacity, and

- providing economic development growth for rural areas and local districts through lease and property tax payments. . . .

A National RPS Will Help Meet Energy Goals

A national RPS is the most direct policy option for Congress to carry out the stated purpose of national energy goals and

RPS Better than Voluntary Approach

The mainstream environmental movement has put a lot of its resources into promoting "green" energy through a market-based approach rather than a public policy approach. The market-based approach is characterized as the voluntary purchasing of "green" power products, which nearly always cost more than buying only conventional power. A public policy approach can take several forms, but usually is done through state or federal laws that provide tax credits or purchasing requirements to "renewable" forms of energy. Purchasing requirements can apply to the state or federal government, requiring them to buy certain types of electricity or they can require sellers of electricity to have a certain percentage of "renewable" power in their mix. The latter type is known as a Renewable Portfolio Standard (RPS). As of September 2007, 26 states have RPS policies as a matter of state law (and 4 others have a "goal"). . . .

The environmental and social damage caused by continued reliance on nuclear power, fossil fuels, hydroelectric dams and "biomass" incineration is extreme. If we're to act with the urgency that these environmental hazards demand, we must pursue strategies that do more than make people feel good while creating comparatively little change. RPS policies have a much larger effect on the energy supply than volunteer purchasing can, even if we get large institutions like colleges and universities to start buying "green" power.

"Promoting Green Energy: The Free Market Approach vs. the Public Policy Approach," Energy Justice Network, *September 2007. www.energyjustice.net.*

fulfill their responsibility to ensure affordable, reliable, secure, and clean sources of energy for the American public.

The energy goals of the U.S. and the Administration have been set forth in the January 2007 State of the Union Address, broadly stated as ensuring "affordable, reliable, secure, and clean sources of energy" and more specifically, the stated purpose of the Energy Policy Act of 2005 was to "help secure our energy future and reduce our dependence on foreign sources of energy by encouraging conservation and efficiency, diversifying our energy supply with alternative and renewable sources, expanding domestic energy production in an environmentally sensitive way, and modernizing our electricity infrastructure."

With a national RPS, Congress can move toward achieving stated national energy goals, and do so while saving American consumers money and providing benefits to the manufacturing sector and rural economies. . . .

The specific purpose of a national RPS is to encourage the widespread use of the nation's abundant renewable resources and install readily available, vastly deployable and cost-effective renewable energy generating capacity to achieve a variety of national energy goals.

The purpose of a national RPS is not specific to any one energy goal or issue facing the market, and the immense value of an RPS as national policy is it will holistically achieve many goals and address a variety of issues simultaneously and cost-effectively. . . .

Addressing global climate change will require broad and integrated energy and environmental policy and a full suite of policy tools. A national RPS is one of the many tools that will be needed. It will serve as a deployment-based policy to ensure that readily available technology is deployed to start immediately avoiding greenhouse gas emissions at a cost savings. Under an economy-wide climate change regulation, each sector will require a unique set of policies to ensure cost-effective greenhouse gas reductions. For the electric sector, an RPS is a necessary and unparalleled policy tool for achieving immediate and cost-effective emission reductions. . . .

How Much Would a National RPS Cost?

Wood Mackenzie, a consultant to the natural gas industry, recently released a report *The Impact of a Federal Renewable Portfolio Standard*. This report analyzed the impact of a 15% national RPS and concluded that the RPS would:

- Reduce variable electricity costs by $240 billion, increase capital investment in electric generation by $134 billion, leading to a net reduction in electricity costs of over $100 million.

- Reduce gas prices at the Henry Hub [natural gas pipeline in Louisiana] from $1.00–1.50/MMBtu [one million British thermal units].

- Reduce wholesale electric power prices by 7–11 percent across the country.

The Department of Energy's Energy Information Administration (EIA) recently released an analysis entitled *Impact of a 15-Percent Renewable Portfolio Standard*. . . .EIA concluded that an RPS would:

- Increase retail electricity prices by a total of less than one percent between 2005 and 2030.

- Reduce natural gas and coal prices.

- Reduce retail natural gas costs by $1 billion between 2005 and 2030.

[And] the Union of Concerned Scientists (UCS) in 2004 analyzed the impact of a 20 percent national RPS and concluded that it would reduce consumer energy (electricity and gas) costs by $49 billion. . . .

RPS Benefits

The Wood Mackenzie report finds that a 15% RPS would avoid nearly 40 percent of CO_2 [carbon dioxide] emission increases in the electric sector and reduce electric sector emissions by nearly 7 percent. EIA finds that a 15% RPS would reduce electric sector CO_2 emissions by 6.7 percent by 2030. The Union of Concerned Scientists finds that a 20% RPS would reduce CO_2 emissions by 15 percent in the electric sector, or avoid nearly 100 percent of the expected emissions increase by 2020. . . .

A national RPS would reduce reliance on imported natural gas, maintain electricity reliability and grid management.

Wood Mackenzie, EIA and the Union of Concerned Scientists all found a reduced demand for natural gas from a national RPS. Foreign imports of natural gas are expected to increase by 25% by 2020, increasing our reliance on foreign fossil fuels. Reducing natural gas demand with renewable energy increases the ability for domestic natural gas resources to meet demand.

An RPS would fit very well with grid reliability goals and grid management. Wind technology in particular is very grid friendly now with power electronics and other new features. High wind penetration now exists in a number of states as well as parts of Europe, and reliability does not present a barrier to further wind development. . . .

A national RPS would require hundreds of thousands of manufacturing and construction jobs, encourage development of new manufacturing facilities in the U.S., and generate millions of dollars in revenue for rural land owners and taxes for local districts. The Union of Concerned Scientists finds that a 20% RPS would generate over 300,000 jobs in manufacturing and construction, and generate over $20 billion in income to farmers, ranchers and rural landowners, as well as new local taxes.

"Unlike a federal RPS mandate, tax incentives for renewables are the most direct and efficient way for the federal government to spur the development of renewable energy resources."

A National Renewable Portfolio Standard Is Not Completely Beneficial

Thomas R. Kuhn

In the following viewpoint, Thomas R. Kuhn argues that a national renewable portfolio standard (RPS) is a bad idea. Many states already have RPS polices, which are based on available resources. Renewable energy isn't available in all parts of the country, says Kuhn, and forcing all utilities to generate an arbitrary percentage of their power by wind and solar would raise electric rates. Kuhn says tax incentives would be more effective than a national RPS. Thomas R. Kuhn is president of the Edison Electric Institute, a Washington-based association of investor-owned electric utilities.

Thomas R. Kuhn, "Renewing Our Sensibility," *The Hill*, July 31, 2007. http://thehill.com. Reproduced by permission.

As you read, consider the following questions:

1. According to Kuhn, requiring utilities to provide 20 percent of their electricity from renewable sources represents how much of an increase over current figures?

2. According to Kuhn, how many states have some form of RPS in place?

3. What two tax credits does Kuhn say have already succeeded in producing renewable energy?

A mericans unquestionably are eager for all industries to introduce more green energy into all that we do, and electric utilities share in that enthusiasm. Utilities from coast to coast are steadily integrating electricity generated from the wind, the sun and other renewable sources into the power they deliver to customers.

20% by 2020 Is Unreasonable

Still, these renewable sources comprise a very modest part of the U.S. electric generation portfolio—slightly less than three percent, in fact. That is just one reason the House of Representatives should reject an amendment. . .that would require most utilities nationwide to provide 20 percent of their electricity from renewable sources by 2020.

That amounts to a roughly 600 percent jump, and in less than 13 years. Such a mandate, or renewable portfolio standard (RPS), will raise power bills for many consumers and create new challenges for maintaining reliable electric service. This is not a sound energy policy.

Of course, everyone wants to use the sun and the wind to make electricity, and our industry is responding. Every U.S. utility with available resources is working diligently to add renewable resources to its generation portfolio, and some companies may well meet or exceed the proposed federal goal.

Renewable Portfolio Standard Impossible to Meet

A federally mandated RPS could raise electricity prices for all consumers, result in a wealth transfer among states, and impose new burdens on the reliability of our nation's electric grid. The Energy Information Administration (EIA) estimates that a 15 percent RPS would require consumers to pay $1 billion to $2 billion more for electricity. Utilities will be forced to purchase renewable energy credits from the federal government, which amounts to a tax on electricity used by businesses and other consumers, driving up energy costs and hurting economic growth. And a mandatory RPS based exclusively on "renewables" chooses energy winners and losers, excluding good, clean energy sources like nuclear, hydroelectric and clean coal for no good reason.

"Letter Opposing the Energy Independence and Security Act of 2007," U.S. Chamber of Commerce, December 5, 2007. www.uschamber.com.

Almost Half the States Have an RPS

In fact, 24 states and the District of Columbia now have some form of RPS in place, each prescribing a varying mix of targets, timetables and fuel choices, depending on what works best for them given their available resources. The proposed federal RPS would conflict with every single one of the state laws, in one way or another.

Some states enjoy a rich abundance of renewable energy sources, including solar energy, geothermal, and vast tracts of windswept desert, but many other states have a distinct paucity of renewable energy resources.

Under the proposed amendment, if utilities cannot generate their own renewable resources, they must buy renewable power from other generators or, more likely, simply write out a check to the federal government to cover the difference. In either outcome, the costs for electricity will be higher, and these costs will be passed along to the customers at a time when overall costs for energy are rising already.

Renewables Are Intermittent

There are other drawbacks to a federal RPS that will impact cost and reliability. Wind and solar energy, of course, are intermittent and do not contribute significantly to electric capacity or reliability. Retail electricity suppliers cannot tell consumers that they will receive electricity only when the wind blows or the sun shines.

Utilities will still need to build generating facilities using conventional fuels—most likely expensive natural gas—to meet consumers' needs for reliable power on short notice, as well as to support their intermittent renewable energy resources. Often overlooked, too, is the challenge of building the new power lines that will be needed to connect wind energy and other renewables from remote areas to population centers, for example. This is a difficult and costly process.

Tax Incentives a Better Idea

House lawmakers do have a very viable "green" alternative to an RPS—they can provide long-term tax incentives to accelerate deployment of renewable energy sources. Unlike a federal RPS mandate, tax incentives for renewables are the most direct and efficient way for the federal government to spur the development of renewable energy resources. The renewables production tax credit (PTC) and the investment tax credit (ITC) for solar and geothermal energy are proven means of actually getting renewable generation built and brought online.

All of us want to put more renewables into our electricity supply. But instead of enacting a top-heavy federal mandate, let's give the states the lead on whether and how to create renewable targets.

"A well designed net metering system is a win-win for. . .utilities and their customers."

Net Metering Programs Are Good Policies

Mona Newton

In the following viewpoint, Mona Newton maintains that net metering can benefit electric utilities, customers, and communities. Net metering allows customers who own small electric generators, such as photovoltaic systems or wind systems, to hook their generators up to the electric grid. When a customer generates more electricity than his or her household can use, the excess is sent to the grid and the electric meter spins backwards. Some electric utilities do not like net metering because they say it hurts their bottom line and their other customers end up paying more. Newton counters these and other arguments against net metering—a policy she says is a win-win for customers and utilities. Mona Newton is a board member of the Colorado Renewable Energy Society (CRES), a nonprofit organization that promotes the economic and environmental benefits of solar, wind, biomass, geothermal, and energy efficiency technologies.

Mona Newton, "Net Metering is a Win-Win for Utilities and Local Communities," Colorado Renewable Energy Society, April 2007. www.cres-energy.org. Reproduced by permission.

As you read, consider the following questions:

1. Why does Newton say that distributed generation can strengthen the distribution grid, especially in rural areas?

2. How many examples of U.S. utilities that have been harmed or claimed to have been harmed by net metering did Newton find?

3. How do utility companies calculate their rates, according to Newton?

As the cost of photovoltaic (PV) systems stabilize and the economics improve every year . . . , homes, ranches, and businesses throughout [Colorado] are buying and installing more PV systems. These homeowners and small businesses make decisions to invest based on costs, financing, and other issues such as hedging against rising electricity prices, etc.

Utilities Have Control over Grid Interconnection

Unfortunately, there is one factor—interconnection with the local utility—that can hinder or help the market economics and can have as much or more impact on the buyer's decision than the market. That factor is the local utility's policy toward interconnecting distributed solar and small wind systems to the grid. Small, distributed generators must have the utility's cooperation or they are dead in the water. This situation exists because the utility is the sole supplier of electricity and, for local electricity generators, the sole buyer. In economic terms, the utility is both a monopoly and a monopsony [a service having only one buyer], with which a solitary customer has no leverage or alternative.

As a result, interconnection rules for utilities are almost always decided in political venues such as state legislatures where agreements can emerge that are fair to both buyers and sellers. This is true for net metering as it was for similar rules before solar and distributed generation came on the scene.

Net Metering Offers Benefits

One method for interconnecting small wind and solar systems has emerged that seems to work better than all the rest: net metering. This is where a homeowner or rancher connects a small PV or wind generating system through the utility meter without installing extra hardware to measure output. The owner gets credit for extra generation against the bill at the same rate the utility charges for use.

There are benefits that accrue to the utility, the customer, and the community from net metering.

For the utility, a well-designed net metering policy provides a simple, low-cost, and easily administered way to deal with distributed generators. Utilities without net metering often have to deal with new distributed generators on a case-by-case basis. This hodge-podge approach can be difficult to manage and can easily lead to misunderstandings.

What about the traditional utility concern of cost and reliability? First, utilities obtain electricity and capacity from small, distributed solar installations. This is electricity they don't have to generate themselves or purchase on the market. For solar systems, this generation takes place every day of the year with a very high correlation with utility peak loads. Utilities call this a high load carrying capability. Of course, small wind systems have a capability value that is much smaller; the wind is variable while sunshine is relatively easy to predict. For both types of systems, utilities obtain the benefit of additional capacity in their service territory paid for by their customers, not by ratepayers.

Distributed generation also can strengthen the distribution grid, especially in rural areas. This is because voltage tends to drop at the end of long distribution lines when loads are high, and if it drops below a threshold level, the breakers will trip and a temporary blackout occurs. Grid-tied solar systems connected to the distribution grid strengthen voltage and improve

State Net Metering Programs Making a Difference

A record number of homeowners and small businesses are declaring their independence from utility monopolies by finding ways to meet their electricity needs more cheaply (and more cleanly) on their own. And more state governments are assuming control of their energy future by intervening to encourage this energy self-reliance.

For nearly 25 years, states have been the crucible for innovative policies to promote small-scale, renewable energy generation. By 2006, 36 states had adopted statewide programs that set rules by which customers who generate their own electricity can interconnect to the central transmission grid. . . .By compensating customers for reducing demand and sharing excess electricity, net metering programs are powerful, market-based incentives that states can use to encourage energy independence.

"Freeing the Grid,"
The Network for New Energy Choices,
November 2006. www.newenergychoices.org.

overall service. And this grid support can defer maintenance and upgrades in the power distribution system, which is a tangible benefit to utilities.

Customers benefit from net metering small wind and solar systems because they obtain a long-term guarantee of low utility bills.

Communities benefit from the investment in local generation. This investment not only increases local property values but increases local business opportunities as well. It is the difference between paying rent and paying a mortgage. Local investment lifts all boats.

Myths About Net Metering

1. Net metering hurts the utility bottom line by reducing revenues. This argument is similar to the one against energy efficiency, that customers reducing their purchases of electricity hurt utility revenues. This would be true if everybody bought a PV system and put it on their roofs.

Unfortunately, there is little risk of this happening. . . .PV is a developing technology that will become cost competitive with conventional generation over a period of many years. The current market is small and does not affect even a fraction of a percentage point on a bottom line of any utility that reports these figures publicly. I cannot find any example of a U.S. utility having been harmed or even claims to be harmed by net metering. . . .

Nevertheless, any net metering policy should receive regular review to monitor progress of the technology and development of the market. The service provided by electric utilities is extremely valuable, and no one that I know wants to hurt that industry. If solar (and especially energy efficiency, which has a much larger potential for impacting rates than solar) gets to the point where it actually reduces utility revenues, I believe rates should be restructured to guarantee that service. After all, solar needs a grid to connect to!

2. Net metering represents a subsidy from one group of customers to another. This argument has to do with the "rate base plus" formula that utilities use to charge customers. The argument is that utilities charge all customers in the same class a single rate, which represents an average cost of doing business plus profit. Under this time-honored formula, all of the differential costs of providing service to individual customers are lumped into a single average cost per kilowatt-hour (kWh). So the person who uses a lot of electricity during the day when the cost of obtaining electricity is higher pays the same as the person who uses all of their electricity at night during off-peak hours. One could argue that one type of consumer "subsidizes" another based on patterns of consumption, etc.

Utilities and their customers have supported this averaging formula for years in the name of economic development. For example, building a new home represents a cost for a utility because it must invest in new generating capacity in order to supply this electricity. Therefore, ratepayers subsidize solar systems through net metering no more than they subsidize construction of new homes. Both represent expanding business opportunities, and electric utilities have figured out a way to accommodate this economic growth through existing rate structures for more than a century.

3. Net metering represents a burden for small utilities. The opposite is actually true because large organizations are better equipped to handle more complicated arrangements. Net metering is as simple as it gets to administer because it requires no special equipment, no new rates to establish, no new procedures. All that is required is that the utility add a line in the ledger for each net metering customer to carry forward credits until the end of the year.

Compare this with the existing alternative for non-utility generators, which requires installation of another meter. Then the utility must make special trips to read this meter and readjust its accounting procedures to keep track of another meter for a single account. All this for measuring small amounts of electricity (in utility terms) from distributed generators. A study by the Pacific Gas & Electric Company in California in 1996 found that the cost of reading the extra meters for distributed PV systems alone outweighed the cost of net metering.

A well designed net metering system is a win-win for. . .utilities and their customers.

> *"Net metering raises important policy issues. . . .Namely, care must be taken to ensure that net metering customers are not overcompensated for their energy sales to utilities."*

Net Metering Programs Could Hurt Electric Utilities

Frank Graves, Philip Hanser, and Greg Basheda for the Edison Electric Institute

In the following viewpoint, Frank Graves, Philip Hanser, and Greg Basheda, writing for the Edison Electric Institute, explain utility company concerns with net metering policies. According to the authors, when a utility company pays net metering customers the full retail rate for their excess electricity, it loses money. The result is that the utility raises rates for other customers and these other customers end up "cross-subsidizing" the net metering customers. The authors believe that net metering customers should not be compensated at the full retail rate. The Edison Electric Institute is an association of shareholder-owned electric companies, which generate 60 percent of the electricity generated in the United States.

Frank Graves, Philip Hanser, and Greg Basheda for the Edison Electric Institute, *PURPA: Making the Sequel Better than the Original*, Washington, DC: Edison Electric Institute, 2006. www.eei.org. Copyright © Edison Electric Institute. Reproduced by permission.

As you read, consider the following questions:

1. According to the authors how many customers were in net metering programs in 2004?
2. At what rate are net meter owners credited for excess power generation, according to a recent survey of state net metering roles?
3. According to the authors, can utilities count on the energy provided by net metering customers to meet its capacity requirements?

Net metering is a simplified method of metering the energy consumed and produced at a home or business that has its own onsite energy generator, such as a small wind turbine or photovoltaic (PV) or solar thermal electric device. Small onsite generators also are known as distributed generation (DG). These generators are owned and operated by retail customers and are used to meet a portion of the customers' demand or to provide backup service for customers that need highly reliable power. Other examples of DG include backup generators at hospitals and combined heat and power systems in industrial plants. The Energy Information Administration (EIA) projects that 5.5 gigawatts [5.5 billion watts] of DG, or slightly less than 2 percent of all new generating capacity, will be installed over the next 25 years.

Net Metering Spins the Meter Backwards

Under net metering, excess electricity produced by the onsite generator will spin the customer's meter "backwards" such that the customer is a net seller of electricity to the local utility at such times. Many states have implemented net metering programs to encourage the use of small, renewable energy systems. Approximately 40 states have adopted some form of net metering law for small wind and/or photovoltaic technologies whereby the customer receives a credit for excess power sold to the utility. While most state net metering programs are open to all retail customers, some states restrict eligibility to particular customer classes. Customer participation in net metering programs has grown significantly. In 2004, a total of 15,286 customers was in net metering programs—a 132 percent increase from 2003. Residential customers accounted for 89 percent of all customers participating in such programs.

Section 1251 of EPAct 2005 [Energy Policy Act of 2005] provides further encouragement for net metering by requiring states to consider whether electric utilities should make net metering service available upon the request of any customer served by the utility at any level. This suggests that almost all electric utilities may need to establish tariffs for net metering service.

Net Metering Raises Concerns

Net metering offers retail customers a convenient and inexpensive way to sell excess energy in quantities that are too small or intermittent to market directly. However, net metering raises important policy issues. . . .Namely, care must be taken to ensure that net metering customers are not overcompensated for their energy sales to utilities; otherwise, customers without DG facilities may end up cross-subsidizing those with onsite generators. Such cross-subsidization could have perverse distributional effects, given that low- and moderate-income consumers would be less likely to install solar panels or renewable generators than high-income customers. Moreover, overpaying net metering customers for their output likely would spur an oversupply of onsite generation, as some customers install technologies solely to take advantage of payments (credits) that exceed the market value of the energy. . . .

Hidden Costs of Full Retail Rate Compensation

Some supporters of net metering argue that customers should receive the full retail rate for any excess power sold to the utility. In other words, if a customer purchases 1,000 kWh [kilo-

Net Metering Negatives

Net metering policies unquestionably subsidize consumers with qualifying generation facilities, and could become burdensome as more qualifying facilities are installed. The policies require utilities to pay consumers retail price for wholesale power. Moreover, the policies require utilities to pay high costs for what is often low-value power. Power from distributed wind and photovoltaic systems is intermittent, cannot be scheduled or dispatched reliably to meet system requirements, and may be expensive in some cases to integrate into the system. . . .

Further, net meters can be deliberately or inadvertently gamed. Consumers can take power from the system at peak times when it costs the utility the most to provide it, and then roll their meters backwards by generating power at non-peak times when the utility has little need for it. That is a particular risk, for example, with wind power. During the hottest days when power demand peaks, wind turbines are often becalmed. The turbines do not begin generating power again until the evenings when the cooler air starts to move in and demand for energy falls.

"White Paper on Distributed Generation,"
National Rural Electric Cooperative Association,
August 2007. www.nreca.org.

watt hours] in a given month at a price of 10 cents/kWh and sells 200 kWh back to the utility, the customer would receive a bill of $80 [800 kWh × 0.10]. Many state regulators have been sympathetic to this argument. A recent survey of state net metering rules shows that most states with such rules credit excess generation at the utility's retail rate rather than at the utility's avoided cost [what it would cost the utility to purchase it from another power company]. . . .

States presumably have been receptive to setting credits for excess generation equal to the utility's retail rate because this is easier for customers to understand—indeed, most small customers probably have no understanding of avoided cost—and it provides incentive for the installation of small renewable energy systems. Such pricing also likely reflects historical metering limitations. . . . However, from an economic perspective, crediting excess generation at the utility's retail rate makes no sense, because retail rates include charges for transmission, distribution, and administrative and overhead costs, not to mention sunk generation costs, and none of these costs, generally speaking, is avoided as a result of excess generation provided by a retail customer. . . .

Paying the full retail rate for any energy provided by net metering customers could lead to significant revenue losses and earnings reductions for utilities. The direct reduction in a utility's revenue from a kWh displaced by net metering (i.e., the retail revenue from that kWh) is offset only by the utility's incremental cost of energy (i.e., the utility's avoided cost). Referring to the earlier example, if the retail rate is 10 cents/kWh, while the utility's incremental cost of energy to serve the customer is 3 cents/kWh, the utility has a net revenue loss of 7 cents/kWh on all energy purchased from the net metering customer. The utility loses 7 cents that would have gone to the recovery of its fixed costs. This lost revenue would have to be collected from other customers by raising their rates or would translate directly into lost earnings for the utility. The impact on a utility's earnings could be significant because of the potentially large gap between its retail rate and its short-term avoided cost, which is the total revenue available per kWh for fixed cost recovery. . . .

Utilities Can't Count on Distributed Generation

Some net metering advocates may argue that these examples are incomplete or misleading because they assume that the utility has sufficient generating capacity. These advocates likely would argue that once this assumption is relaxed, the cross-subsidy problem goes away because onsite generators help the utility avoid capacity costs. There are two problems with this argument. First, . . .the timing and quantity of energy provided by net metering customers is uncertain. Nor are such customers under any obligation to provide specified quantities of power to the local utility at specified times. Thus, even if a utility does need additional capacity, it is questionable as to whether net metering customers will enable the utility to avoid or defer the construction of new generating capacity. Simply put, the energy provided by net metering customers is not a "firm" supply source that a utility can count on to meet its capacity requirements.

When Utilities Lose, Other Ratepayers Foot the Bill

Second, even if onsite generators collectively do enable the utility to avoid or defer the construction of additional generation (and/or local distribution) capacity, the cross-subsidy problem does not necessarily go away. To the extent that the retail rate that the net metering customer receives for its output exceeds the utility's avoided cost, including the incremental cost of avoided capacity, the utility continues to overpay for this power and lose a contribution to its fixed costs. This lost revenue will have to be recovered from other ratepayers or will result in reduced earnings for shareholders.

Periodical Bibliography

The following articles have been selected to supplement the diverse views presented in this chapter.

Bruce Barcott	"Green Tags: Making Sense of the REC-Age," *World Watch.* July–August 2007.
Coral Davenport	"A Clean Break in Energy Policy," *CQ Weekly.* October 8, 2007.
Bob Dinneen	"RFA's Bob Dinneen Discusses Renewable Fuels Standard," *E & E Daily.* February 14, 2008.
David M. Herszenhorn	"House Passes Renewable Energy Credits," *New York Times.* February 28, 2008.
Edward Krapels	"Mercantilism and the Green Energy Debate," *Boston Globe.* March 3, 2008.
Newsweek	"Force of Nature: Environmentalism Is No Longer the Province of the Left," August 14, 2006.
North Carolina State University	"Database of State Incentives for Renewables and Efficiency," *NCSU.* www.dsireusa.org.
Rapid City Journal	"Net Metering Good Energy Policy," February 11, 2008.
Fred Sissine	"Renewable Energy Portfolio Standard (RPS): Background and Debate Over a National Requirement," *Congressional Research Service Reports.* August 6, 2007.
Benjamin K. Sovacool and Jack N. Barkenbus	"Necessary but Insufficient: State Renewable Portfolio Standards and Climate Change Policies," *Environment.* July–August 2007.
Stephen Spruiell	"Farmers on the Dole: The Crying Need for Ag Reform," *National Review.* August 13, 2007.
Rosalie Westenskow	"Analysis: New RFS Law Already Under Fire," *United Press International.* February 8, 2008.

For Further Discussion

Chapter 1

1. Gia Milinovich says that nuclear power is renewable, while the Pembina Institute says it is not. How do you think each author weighs the problems associated with nuclear waste in deciding whether or not nuclear power is renewable? Explain.

2. Nickolas J. Themelis and Karsten Millrath argue that municipal solid waste is renewable and it is wasteful not to use it for energy production. But Peter Montague maintains that garbage is not renewable. Montague says that if we use garbage for energy it will encourage Americans to produce more garbage, rather than less. Which viewpoint do you agree with and why? If you knew that your garbage was being used to produce energy, do you think it would influence your behavior?

3. Martha T. Moore discusses the benefits of using animal manure to generate energy. The Sierra Club opposes such use of animal manure, claiming it will encourage the construction of more factory farms. Do you think the Sierra Club is correct in their assertion that support for "methane digesters" amounts to support for concentrated animal feeding operations (CAFOS)? Why or why not?

Chapter 2

1. Al Gore believes climate change poses a grave threat to humanity. How do you rate the threat from climate change or global warming? Support your answer.

2. Roger Bezdek, consulting for the American Solar Energy Society, thinks that the government should invest in renewable energy. However, the Independence Institute be-

lieves government investment in renewable energy is too costly. How do you think the mission of each organization influences its viewpoint? Explain.

Chapter 3

1. The Natural Resources Defense Council and Climate Solutions believe ethanol is a good substitute for gasoline. However, Ed Wallace believes it is not. Describe how each supports their viewpoint? Does each provide supporting evidence? Can you see any difference between the types of supporting evidence they provide?

2. Diane Greer talks about the benefits of cellulosic ethanol, one of which is that it can enhance the nation's energy security. However, Alice Friedemann finds cellulosic ethanol unsustainable and a threat to energy security. Specifically, what reason does Greer give for saying cellulosic ethanol can increase energy security? Why does Friedemann say cellulosic ethanol is a threat to energy security?

3. Lester R. Brown believes that shifting corn from food to fuel will lead to a food crisis in developing countries. However, Patrick Mazza believes this is an exaggerated claim. Is there anything that Brown or Mazza agree upon? If so, what is it?

Chapter 4

1. Jaime Steve thinks the government should a adopt a national renewable portfolio standard (RPS), while Thomas R. Kuhn thinks there are better ways to encourage renewable energy. What do you think Steve and Kuhn might think about a renewable fuels standard (RFS)? What are the differences between an RPS and an RFS?

2. Mona Newton maintains that governments should adopt net metering policies because they provide benefits to the public good, while Frank Graves, Philip Hanser, and Greg

Basheda say that net metering is costly to other customers. Do you think that net metering should be allowed even if it is subsidized by other customers? Explain why or why not.

Organizations to Contact

The editors have compiled the following list of organizations concerned with the issues debated in this book. The descriptions are derived from materials provided by the organizations. All have publications or information available for interested readers. The list was compiled on the date of publication of the present volume; the information provided here may change. Readers need to remember that many organizations take several weeks or longer to respond to inquiries.

American Wind Energy Association
1101 14th Street NW, 12th Floor, Washington, DC   20005
(202) 383-2500 • fax: (202) 383-2505
e-mail: windmail@awea.org
Web site: www.awea.org

The American Wind Energy Association (AWEA) is a national trade organization representing the wind power industry. The organization promotes wind energy as a clean source of electricity for consumers around the world. The AWEA provides up-to-date information on wind energy companies and projects, new technology, and policy developments related to wind and other renewable energy development. AWEA publishes the weekly and monthly newsletters, *Wind Energy Weekly* and *Windletter.*

The Edison Foundation and the Edison Electric Institute
701 Pennsylvania Ave. NW, Washington, DC   20004-2695
(for EF)(202) 347-5878
Web sites: www.edisonfoundation.net and www.eei.org

The Edison Foundation (EF) is a nonprofit organization promoting the benefits of electricity. The foundation works to encourage a greater understanding of the production, delivery, and use of electric power, and supports its mission through research, conferences, grants, and other outreach activities.

The Edison Electric Institute (EEI) is an association of U.S. shareholder-owned electric companies. Organized in 1933, EEI provides information about the U.S. electric industry and works to advocate for the industry. EEI publishes a periodical magazine, called *Electric Perspectives*.

Electric Power Research Institute
3420 Hillview Ave., Palo Alto, CA   94304
(650) 855-2000
e-mail: askepri@epri.com
Web site: http://my.epri.com

The Electric Power Research Institute (EPRI) is an independent, nonprofit center for public interest energy and environmental research. EPRI works collaboratively with leading experts in the electric industry to find solutions to the challenges of electric power. The *EPRI Journal* published by the organization reports on and provides insight into energy issues. EPRI has several U.S. offices in addition to the one given above.

Energy Information Administration
1000 Independence Ave. SW, Washington, DC   20585
(202) 586-8800
e-mail: InfoCtr@eia.doe.gov
Web site: www.eia.doe.gov

The Energy Information Administration (EIA), created by Congress in 1977, is the statistical agency of the U.S. Department of Energy. The EIA's mission is to provide objective energy data, energy forecasts, and analyses to promote sound policy making, efficient energy markets, and to promote public understanding of energy and its interaction with the economy and the environment. The agency's Web site has an "Energy 101" page, a "Frequently Asked Questions" page, and an "Energy Kids Page." The EIA publishes a number of energy reports, such as a national energy profile, state energy profiles, international energy profiles, and annual and monthly forecasts of all energy sectors.

Heartland Institute
19 South LaSalle St., Suite 903, Chicago, IL 60603
(312) 377-4000
e-mail: think@heartland.org
Web site: www.heartland.org

The Heartland Institute is a national nonprofit research and education organization. The organization's mission is to discover, develop, and promote free-market solutions to social and economic problems including those affecting climate and energy. The Heartland Institute produces five monthly publications, including the *Environment & Climate News*. The organization also publishes policy studies and books, and hosts conferences and other events.

National Renewable Energy Laboratory
1617 Cole Blvd., Golden, CO 80401-3393
(303) 275-3000
Web site: www.nrel.gov

The National Renewable Energy Laboratory (NREL) is the U.S. government's primary laboratory for renewable energy and energy efficiency research and development. NREL's mission is to develop renewable energy and energy efficiency technologies and practices to address the nation's energy and environmental goals. NREL works to bring new renewable energy technologies from the laboratory to the marketplace. NREL's Web site includes a student resource page. The agency also publishes *Discover NREL*, a bimonthly newsletter.

Office of Energy Efficiency and Renewable Energy
Mail Stop EE-1, Department of Energy
1000 Independence Ave. SW, Washington, DC 20585
(877) 337-3463
Web site: www.eere.energy.gov

The Energy Efficiency and Renewable Energy Office (EERE) is a department of the U.S. Department of Energy (DOE). The EERE seeks to help the DOE achieve its goals of strengthening

America's energy security, environmental quality, and economic vitality. The EERE works to enhance energy efficiency and productivity and bring clean, reliable and affordable energy technologies to the marketplace. The EERE publishes several newsletters such as, *Energy Matters, Conservation Update,* and *EERE Network News.*

Renewable Energy Policy Project

1612 K St. NW, Suite 202, Washington, DC   20006
(202) 293-2898 • fax: (202) 293-5857
e-mail: gsterzinger@repp.org
Web site: http://crest.org

The goal of the Renewable Energy Policy Project is to accelerate the use of renewable energy by providing credible information, policy analysis, and innovative strategies. The group supports research, disseminates information, and facilitates renewable energy discussions. The organization publishes reports and studies about renewable energy.

Renewable Fuels Association

One Massachusetts Ave. NW, Suite 820
Washington, DC   20001
(202) 289-3835
Web site: www.ethanolrfa.org

The Renewable Fuels Association (RFA) is a national trade association for the U.S. ethanol industry. The RFA promotes policies, regulations, and research and development initiatives that will lead to the increased production and use of fuel ethanol. The organization publishes an annual industry outlook, ethanol facts, and various reports and studies.

Sierra Club

85 Second St., 2nd Floor, San Francisco, CA   94105
(415) 977-5500 • fax: (415) 977-5799
e-mail: information@sierraclub.org
Web site: www.sierraclub.org

The Sierra Club, established in 1892, is one of the oldest environmental organizations in the United States. The organization seeks to protect the wild places of the Earth, practice and promote the responsible use of the Earth's ecosystems and resources, and educate the public to protect and restore the quality of the natural and human environment. The Sierra Club publishes the magazine *Sierra*, the *Sierra Club Bulletin*, and the electronic newsletter, *Insider*.

The Sustainable Energy Coalition
6930 Carroll Ave., Suite 340, Takoma Park, MD   20912
Web site: www.sustainableenergycoalition.org

The Sustainable Energy Coalition (SEC) is a consortium of national and state-level business, environmental, consumer, and energy policy organizations. Founded in 1992, it promotes increased federal support for energy efficiency and renewable energy technologies, and reduced federal support for unsafe or polluting energy resources. The organization's Web site provides facts, sustainability studies, and articles about renewable energy.

Union of Concerned Scientists
2 Brattle Square, Cambridge, MA   02238-9105
(617) 547-5552 • fax: (617) 864-9405
Web site: www.ucsusa.org

The Union of Concerned Scientists (UCS) is a nonprofit organization that conducts independent scientific research and promotes citizen action to develop innovative, practical solutions to national problems and issues. It also works to secure responsible changes in government policy, corporate practices, and consumer choices. The organization addresses a range of issues, from global warming and the dangers of nuclear weapons to vehicle pollution and the risks of genetically engineered food crops. UCS publishes reports on global warming, clean energy, and other issues, as well as a monthly magazine, *Catalyst*, and a newsletter, *Earthwise*.

Bibliography of Books

Lester R. Brown   *Plan B 2.0: Rescuing a Planet Under Stress and a Civilization in Trouble.* New York: W.W. Norton & Company, 2006.

Aldo Viero Da Rosa   *Fundamentals of Renewable Energy Processes.* Boston: Elsevier Academic Press, 2005.

Mark E. Eberhart   *Feeding the Fire: The Lost History and Uncertain Future of Mankind's Energy Addiction.* New York: Harmony Books, 2007.

Robert L. Evans   *Fueling Our Future: An Introduction to Sustainable Energy.* New York: Cambridge University Press, 2007.

Tim F. Flannery   *The Weather Makers: How Man Is Changing the Climate and What It Means for Life on Earth.* New York: Atlantic Monthly Press, 2005.

Stan Gibilisco   *Alternative Energy Demystified.* New York: McGraw-Hill, 2007.

Chris Goodall   *How to Live a Low-Carbon Life: The Individual's Guide to Stopping Climate Change.* Sterling, VA: Earthscan, 2007.

Lindsey Grant   *The Collapsing Bubble: Growth and Fossil Energy.* Santa Ana, CA: Seven Locks Press, 2005.

Richard Heinberg   *The Party's Over: Oil, War and the Fate of Industrial Societies.* Gabriola Island, BC: New Society Publishers, 2005.

Dilip Hiro   *Blood of the Earth: The Battle for the World's Vanishing Oil Resources.* New York: Nation Books, 2007.

Peter W. Huber and Mark P. Mills   *The Bottomless Well: The Twilight of Fuel, the Virtue of Waste, and Why We Will Never Run Out of Energy.* New York: Basic Books, 2005.

Jay Inslee and Bracken Hendricks   *Apollo's Fire: Igniting America's Clean-Energy Economy.* Washington, DC: Island Press, 2008.

Mark Jaccard   *Sustainable Fossil Fuels: The Unusual Suspect in the Quest for Clean and Enduring Energy.* Vancouver, BC: Simon Fraser University, 2006.

David Jefferis   *Green Power: Eco-Energy Without Pollution.* New York: Crabtree Publishing, 2006.

Regina Anne Kelly   *Energy Supply and Renewable Resources.* New York: Facts On File, 2007.

Paul Komor   *Renewable Energy Policy.* Lincoln, NE: iUniverse, Inc., 2004.

Paul Kruger   *Alternative Energy Resources: The Quest for Sustainable Energy.* Hoboken, NJ: John Wiley, 2006.

James Howard Kunstler
The Long Emergency: Surviving the Converging Catastrophes of the Twenty-First Century. New York: Atlantic Monthly Press, 2005.

Volkmar Lauber
Switching to Renewable Power: A Framework for the 21st Century. Sterling, VA: Earthscan, 2005.

Amory B. Lovins
Winning the Oil Endgame: Innovation for Profits, Jobs, and Security. Snowmass, CO: Rocky Mountain Institute, 2004.

Andrew McKillop and Sheila Newman
The Final Energy Crisis. Ann Arbor, MI: Pluto, 2005.

Greg Pahl
Biodiesel: Growing a New Energy Economy. White River Junction, VT: Chelsea Green Publishing, 2005.

Hermann Scheer
Energy Autonomy: The Economic, Social and Technological Case for Renewable Energy. Sterling, VA: Earthscan, 2007.

Christopher Simon
Alternative Energy: Political, Economic, and Social Feasibility. Lanham, MD: Rowman & Littlefield Publishers, 2007.

Darlene Stille
Natural Resources: Using and Protecting Earth's Supplies. Minneapolis, MN: Compass Point Books, 2005.

William Sweet — *Kicking the Carbon Habit: Global Warming and the Case for Renewable and Nuclear Energy.* New York: Columbia University Press, 2006.

Peter Tertzakian — *A Thousand Barrels a Second: The Coming Oil Break Point and the Challenges Facing an Energy Dependent World.* New York: McGraw-Hill, 2007.

Jefferson W. Tester — *Sustainable Energy: Choosing Among Options.* Cambridge, MA: MIT Press, 2005.

Ted Trainer — *Renewable Energy Cannot Sustain a Consumer Society.* New York: Springer, 2007.

Wendy Williams and Robert Whitcomb — *Cape Wind: Money, Celebrity, Class, Politics, and the Battle for Our Energy Future on Nantucket Sound.* New York: PublicAffairs, 2007.

Worldwatch Institute — *American Energy: The Renewable Path to Energy Security.* Washington, DC: Worldwatch Institute, 2006.

Index